Charles Kingsley

Discipline and other Sermons

Charles Kingsley

Discipline and other Sermons

ISBN/EAN: 9783743317994

Manufactured in Europe, USA, Canada, Australia, Japa

Cover: Foto ©Lupo / pixelio.de

Manufactured and distributed by brebook publishing software (www.brebook.com)

Charles Kingsley

Discipline and other Sermons

DISCIPLINE

AND OTHER SERMONS

BY

CHARLES KINGSLEY

London
MACMILLAN AND CO., Limited
NEW YORK: THE MACMILLAN COMPANY
1899

All rights reserved

RICHARD CLAY AND SONS, LIMITED,
LONDON AND BUNGAY.

First Edition (Fcap. 8vo, 6s.), 1867.
Reduced in 1871 *to* 3s. 6d. ; *Reprinted* 1874 ;
Reprinted (Crown 8vo), 1881, 1884, 1888, 1890, 1899.

CONTENTS.

SERMON	PAGE
I. Discipline	1
II. The Temple of Wisdom	11
III. Prayer and Science	23
IV. God's Training	40
V. Good Friday	50
VI. False Civilization	62
VII. The Name of God	75
VIII. The End of Religion	92
IX. The Humanity of God	103
X. God's World	112
XI. The Armour of God	125
XII. Paul and Felix	140
XIII. The Good Samaritan	154
XIV. Consider the Lilies of the Field	168

SERMON	PAGE
XV. THE JEWISH REBELLIONS	184
XVI. TERROR BY NIGHT	198
XVII. THE SON OF THUNDER	212
XVIII. HUMILITY	225
XIX. A WHITSUN SERMON	237
XX. SELF-HELP	250
XXI. ENDURANCE	259
XXII. TOLERATION	274
XXIII. THE KINGDOM OF CHRIST	290
XXIV. THE LIKENESS OF GOD	303

DISCIPLINE,

AND OTHER SERMONS.

SERMON I.

DISCIPLINE.

(*Preached at the Volunteer Camp, Wimbledon, July* 14, 1867.)

NUMBERS XXIV. 9.

He couched, he lay down as a lion; and as a great lion. Who dare rouse him up?

THESE were the words of the Eastern sage, as he looked down from the mountain height upon the camp of Israel, abiding among the groves of the lowland, according to their tribes, in order, discipline, and unity. Before a people so organized, he saw well, none of the nations round could stand. Israel would burst through them, with the strength of the wild bull crashing through the forest. He would couch as a lion, and as a great lion. Who dare rouse him up?

But such a people, the wise Balaam saw, would not be mere conquerors, like those savage hordes, or plundering armies, which have so often swept over the earth before and since, leaving no trace behind save blood and ashes. Israel would be not only a conqueror, but a colonist and a civilizer. And as the sage looked down on that well-ordered camp, he seems to have forgotten for a moment that every man therein was a stern and practised warrior. 'How goodly,' he cries, 'are thy 'tents, oh Jacob, and thy camp, oh Israel.' He likens them, not to the locust swarm, the sea flood, nor the forest fire, but to the most peaceful, and most fruitful sights in nature or in art. They are spread forth like the watercourses, which carry verdure and fertility as they flow. They are planted like the hanging gardens beside his own river Euphrates, with their aromatic shrubs and wide-spreading cedars. Their God-given mission may be stern, but it will be beneficent. They will be terrible in war; but they will be wealthy, prosperous, civilized and civilizing, in peace.

Many of you must have seen—all may see

—that noble picture of Israel in Egypt which now hangs in the Royal Academy; in which the Hebrews, harnessed like beasts of burden, writhing under the whips of their taskmasters, are dragging to its place some huge Egyptian statue.

Compare the degradation portrayed in that picture with this prophecy of Balaam's, and then consider—What, in less than two generations, had so transformed those wretched slaves?

Compare, too, with Balaam's prophecy the hints of their moral degradation which Scripture gives;—the helplessness, the hopelessness, the cowardice, the sensuality, which cried, 'Let us alone, that we may serve the 'Egyptians. Because there were no graves 'in Egypt, hast thou brought us forth to die 'in the wilderness?' 'Whose highest wish 'on earth was to sit by the fleshpots of 'Egypt, where they did eat bread to the full.' What had transformed that race into a lion, whom none dare rouse up?

Plainly, those forty years of freedom. But of freedom under a stern military education:

of freedom chastened by discipline, and organized by law.

I say, of freedom. No nation of those days, we have reason to believe, enjoyed a freedom comparable to that of the old Jews. They were, to use our modern phrase, the only constitutional people of the East. The burdensomeness of Moses' law, ere it was overlaid, in later days, by Rabbinical scrupulosity, has been much exaggerated. In its simpler form, in those early times, it left every man free to do, as we are expressly told, that which was right in his own eyes, in many most important matters. Little seems to have been demanded of the Jews, save those simple ten commandments, which we still hold to be necessary for all civilized society.

And their obedience was, after all, a moral obedience; the obedience of free hearts and wills. The law could threaten to slay them for wronging each other; but they themselves had to enforce the law against themselves. They were always physically strong enough to defy it, if they chose. They did not defy it, because they believed in it, and felt that in obedience and loyalty lay the salvation of themselves and of their race.

It was not, understand me, the mere physical training of these forty years which had thus made them men indeed. Whatever they may have gained by that—the younger generation at least—of hardihood, endurance, and self-help, was a small matter compared with the moral training which they had gained—a small matter, compared with the habits of obedience, self-restraint, self-sacrifice, mutual trust, and mutual help; the inspiration of a common patriotism, of a common national destiny. Without that moral discipline, they would have failed each other in need; have broken up, scattered, or perished, or at least remained as settlers or as slaves among the Arab tribes. With that moral discipline, they held together, and continued one people till the last, till they couched, they lay down as a lion, and as a great lion, and none dare rouse them up.

You who are here to-day—I speak to those in uniform—are the representatives of more than one great body of your countrymen, who have determined to teach themselves something of that lesson which Israel learnt in the wilderness; not indeed by actual danger and actual need, but by preparation for dangers and for needs, which are only too possible as long as there is sin upon this earth.

I believe—I have already seen enough to be sure—that your labour and that of your comrades will not be in vain; that you will be, as you surely may be, the better men for that discipline to which you have subjected yourselves.

You must never forget that there are two sides, a softer and a sterner side, to the character of the good man; that he, the perfect Christ, who is the Lion of Judah, taking vengeance, in every age, on all who wrong their fellow men, is also the Lamb of God, who shed his own blood for those who rebelled against him. You must recollect that there are virtues—graces we call them rather—which you may learn elsewhere better than in the camp or on the drilling ground; graces of character more devout, more pure, more tender, more humane, yet necessary for the perfect man, which you will learn rather in your own homes, from the innocence of your own children, from the counsels and examples of your mothers and your wives.

But there are virtues—graces we must call them too—just as necessary for the perfect man, which your present training ought to foster as (for most of you) no other training can; virtues which the old monk tried to teach by the stern education of the cloister; which are still taught, thank God, by the stern education of our public schools; which you and your comrades may learn by the best of all methods, by teaching them to yourselves.

For here, and wherever military training goes on, must be kept in check those sins of self-will, conceit, self-indulgence, which beset all free and prosperous men. Here must be practised virtues which (if not the very highest) are yet virtues still, and will be such to all eternity.

For the moral discipline which goes to make a good soldier or a successful competitor on this ground,—the self-restraint, the obedience, the diligence, the punctuality, the patience, the courtesy, the forbearance, the justice, the temperance,—these virtues, needful for those who compete in a struggle in which the idler and the debauchee can take no share, all these go equally toward the making of a good man.

The germs of these virtues you must bring hither with you. And none can give them to you save the Spirit of God, the giver of all good. But here you may have them, I trust, quickened into more active life, strengthened into more settled habits, to stand you in good stead in all places, all circumstances, all callings; whether you shall go to serve your country and your family, in trade or agriculture, at home; or whether you shall go forth, as many of you will, as soldiers, colonists, or merchants, to carry English speech and English civilization to the ends of all the earth.

For then, if you learn to endure hardness—in plain English, to exercise obedience and self-restraint—will you be (whether regulars or civilians) alike the soldiers of Christ, able and willing to fight in that war of which He is the Supreme Commander, and which will endure as long as there is darkness and misery upon the earth; even the battle of the living God against the baser instincts of our nature, against ignorance and folly, against lawlessness and tyranny, against brutality and sloth. Those, the deadly enemies of the human race, you are all bound to attack, if you be good men and true, wheresoever you shall meet them invading the kingdom of your Saviour and your God. But you can only conquer them in others in proportion as you have conquered them in yourselves.

May God give you grace to conquer them in yourselves more and more; to profit by the discipline which you may gain by this movement; and bequeath it, as a precious heirloom, to your children hereafter!

For so, whether at home or abroad, will you help to give your nation that moral strength, without which physical strength is mere violent weakness; and by the example and influence of your own discipline, obedience, and self-restraint, help to fulfil of your own nation the prophecy of the Seer—

'He couched, he lay down as a lion; and as a great lion. Who dare rouse him up?'

SERMON I

THE TEMPLE OF WISDOM.

(Preached at Wellington College, All Saints' Day, 1866.)

PROVERBS IX. 1—5.

Wisdom hath builded her house, she hath hewn out her seven pillars: she hath killed her beasts; she hath mingled her wine; she hath also furnished her table. She hath sent forth her maidens; she crieth upon the highest places of the city, Whoso is simple, let him turn in hither: and to him that wanteth understanding, she saith to him, Come, eat of my bread, and drink of the wine which I have mingled.

THIS allegory has been a favourite one with many deep and lofty thinkers. They mixed it, now and then, with Greek fancies; and brought Phœbus, Apollo, and the Muses into the Temple of Wisdom. But whatever they added to the allegory, they always preserved the allegory itself. No words, they felt, could so well express what Wisdom was, and how it was to be obtained by man.

The stately Temple, built by mystic rules of art; the glorious Lady, at once its Architect, its Priestess, and its Queen; the feast spread within for all who felt in themselves divine aspirations after what is beautiful, and good, and true; the maidens fair and pure, sent forth throughout the city, among the millions intent only on selfish gain or selfish pleasure, to call in all who were not content to be only a more crafty kind of animal, that they might sit down at the feast among the noble company of guests,—those who have inclined their heart to wisdom, and sought for understanding as for hid treasures:—this is a picture which sages and poets felt was true; true for all men, and for all lands. And it will be, perhaps, looked on as true once more, as natural, all but literally exact, when we who are now men are in our graves, and you who are now boys will be grown men; in the days when the present soulless mechanical notion of the world and of men shall have died out, and philosophers shall see once more that Wisdom is no discovery of their own, but the inspiration of the Almighty; and that this world is no dead and dark machine, but alight with the Glory, and alive with the Spirit, of God.

But what has this allegory, however true, to do with All Saints' Day?

My dear boys, on all days Wisdom calls you to her feast, by many weighty arguments, by many loving allurements, by many awful threats. But on this day, of all the year, she calls you by the memory of the example of those who sit already and for ever at her feast. By the memory and example of the wise of every age and every land, she bids you enter in and feast with them, on the wealth which she, and they, her faithful servants, have prepared for you. They have laboured; and they call you, in their mistress's name, to enter into their labours. She taught them wisdom, and she calls on you to learn wisdom of them in turn.

Remember, I say, this day, with humility and thankfulness of heart, the wise who are gone home to their rest.

There are many kinds of noble personages amid the blessed company of All Saints, whom

I might bid you to remember this day. Some of you are the sons of statesmen or lawyers. I might call on you to thank God for your fathers, and for every man who has helped to make or execute wise laws. Some of you are the sons of soldiers. I might call on you to thank God for your fathers, and for all who have fought for duty and for their country's right. Some of you are the sons of clergymen. I might call on you to thank God for your fathers, and for all who have preached the true God and Jesus Christ His only-begotten Son, whether at home or abroad. All of you have mothers, whether on earth or in heaven; I might call on you to thank God for them, and for every good and true woman who, since the making of the world, has raised the coarseness and tamed the fierceness of men into gentleness and reverence, purity, and chivalry. I might do this: but to-day I will ask you to remember specially—The Wise.

For you are here as scholars; you are here to learn wisdom; you are here in what should be, and I believe surely is, one of the forecourts of that mystic Temple into which

Wisdom calls us all. And therefore it is fit that you should this day remember the wise; for they have laboured, and you are entering into their labours. Every lesson which you learn in school, all knowledge which raises you above the savage or the profligate (who is but a savage dressed in civilized garments), has been made possible to you by the wise. Every doctrine of theology, every maxim of morals, every rule of grammar, every process of mathematics, every law of physical science, every fact of history or of geography, which you are taught here, is a voice from beyond the tomb. Either the knowledge itself, or other knowledge which led to it, is an heirloom to you from men whose bodies are now mouldering in the dust, but whose spirits live for ever before God, and whose works follow them, going on, generation after generation, upon the path which they trod while they were upon earth, the path of usefulness, as lights to the steps of youth and ignorance. They are the salt of the earth, which keeps the world of man from decaying back into barbarism. They are the children of light whom God has set for lights that cannot be hid. They are the aristocracy of God, into which not many noble, not many rich, not many mighty are called. Most of them were poor; many all but unknown in their own time; many died, and saw no fruit of their labours; some were persecuted, some were slain, even as Christ the Lord was slain, as heretics, innovators, and corruptors of youth. Of some, the very names are forgotten. But though their names be dead, their works live, and grow, and spread, over ever fresh generations of youth, showing them fresh steps toward that Temple of Wisdom, which is the knowledge of things as they are; the knowledge of those eternal laws by which God governs the heavens and the earth, things temporal and eternal, physical and spiritual, seen and unseen, from the rise and fall of mighty nations, to the growth and death of the moss on yonder moors.

They made their mistakes; they had their sins; for they were men of like passions with ourselves. But this they did—They cried after Wisdom, and lifted up their voice for understanding; they sought for her as silver, and searched for her as hid treasure: and not in vain.

For them, as to every earnest seeker after wisdom, that Heavenly Lady showed herself and her exceeding beauty; and gave gifts to each according to his earnestness, his purity and his power of sight.

To some she taught moral wisdom—righteousness, and justice, and equity, yea, every good path.

To others she showed that political science, which—as Solomon tells you—is but another side of her beauty, and cannot be parted, however men may try, from moral wisdom—that Wisdom in whose right hand is length of days, and in her left hand riches and honour; whose ways are ways of pleasantness, and all her paths are peace.

To others again she showed that physical science which—so Solomon tells us again—cannot be parted safely from the two others. For by the same wisdom, he says, which gives alike righteousness and equity, riches and long life—by that same wisdom, and no other, did the Lord found the heavens and establish the earth; by that same knowledge of his are the depths broken up, and the clouds drop down the dew.

And to some she showed herself, as she did to good Boethius in his dungeon, in the deepest vale of misery, and the hour of death; when all seemed to have deserted them, save Wisdom, and the God from whom she comes; and bade them be of good cheer still, and keep innocency, and take heed to the thing that is right, for that shall bring a man peace at the last.

And they beheld her, and loved her, and obeyed her, each according to his powers: and now they have their reward.

And what is their reward?

How can I tell, dear boys? This, at least can I say, for Scripture has said it already. That God is merciful in this; that he rewardeth every man according to his work. This, at least, I can say, for God incarnate himself has said it already—that to the good and faithful servant he will say,—'Well 'done. Thou hast been faithful over a few 'things: I will make thee ruler over many

'things. Enter thou into the joy of thy
'Lord.'

'The joy of thy Lord.' Think of these words a while. Perhaps they may teach us something of the meaning of All Saints' Day.

For, if Jesus Christ be—as he is—the same yesterday, to-day, and for ever, then his joy now must be the same as his joy was when he was here on earth,—to do good, and to behold the fruit of his own goodness; to see —as Isaiah prophesied of him—to see of the travail of his soul, and be satisfied.

And so it may be; so it surely is—with them; if blessed spirits (as I believe) have knowledge of what goes on on earth. They enter into the joy of their Lord. Therefore they enter into the joy of doing good. They see of the travail of their soul, and are satisfied that they have not lived in vain. They see that their work is going on still on earth; that they, being dead, yet speak, and call ever fresh generations into the Temple of Wisdom.

My dear boys, take this one thought away

with you from this chapel to-day. Believe that the wise and good of every age and clime are looking down on you, to see what use you will make of the knowledge which they have won for you. Whether they laboured, like Kepler in his garret, or like Galileo in his dungeon, hid in God's tabernacle from the strife of tongues; or, like Socrates and Plato, in the whirl and noise—far more wearying and saddening than any loneliness—of the foolish crowd, they all have laboured for you. Let them rejoice, when they see you enter into their labours with heart and soul. Let them rejoice, when they see in each one of you one of the fairest sights on earth, before men and before God; a docile and innocent boy striving to become a wise and virtuous man.

And whenever you are tempted to idleness and frivolity; whenever you are tempted to profligacy and low-mindedness; whenever you are tempted—as you will be too often in these mean days—to join the scorners and the fools whom Solomon denounced; tempted to sneering unbelief in what is great and good, what is laborious and self-sacrificing, and to the fancy that you were sent into this world merely to get through it agreeably;—then fortify and ennoble your hearts by Solomon's vision. Remember who you are, and where you are—that you stand before the Temple of Wisdom, of the science of things as God has made them; wherein alone is health and wealth for body and for soul; that from within the Heavenly Lady calls to you, sending forth her handmaidens in every art and science which has ever ministered to the good of man; and that within there await you all the wise and good who have ever taught on earth, that you may enter in and partake of the feast which their mistress taught them to prepare. Remember, I say, who you are— even the sons of God; and remember where you are—for ever upon sacred ground; and listen with joy and hope to the voice of the Heavenly Wisdom, as she calls—'Whoso is ' simple, let him come in hither; and him that ' wanteth understanding, let him come and ' eat of my bread, and drink of the wine that ' I have mingled.'

Listen with joy and hope: and yet with fear and trembling, as of Moses when he hid his face, for he was afraid to look upon God. For the voice of Wisdom is none other than the voice of The Spirit of God, in whom you live, and move, and have your being.

SERMON III.

PRAYER AND SCIENCE.

(*Preached at St. Olave's Church, Hart Street, before the Honourable Corporation of the Trinity House,* 1866.)

PSALM CVII. 23, 24, 28.

They that go down to the sea in ships, that do business in great waters; these see the works of the Lord, and his wonders in the deep. . . . . Then they cry unto the Lord in their trouble, and he bringeth them out of their distresses.

THESE are days in which there is much dispute about religion and science—how far they agree with each other; whether they contradict or interfere with each other. Especially there is dispute about Providence. Men say, and truly, that the more we look into the world, the more we find everything governed by fixed and regular laws; that man is bound to find out those laws, and save himself from danger by science and experience. But they go on to say,—'And 'therefore there is no use in prayer. You 'cannot expect God to alter the laws of His 'universe because you ask Him: the world 'will go on, and ought to go on, its own way; 'and the man who prays against danger, by 'sea or land, is asking vainly for that which 'will not be granted him.'

Now I cannot see why we should not allow,—what is certainly true,—that the world moves by fixed and regular laws: and yet allow at the same time,—what I believe is just as true,—that God's special providence watches over all our actions, and that, to use our Lord's example, not a sparrow falls to the ground without some special reason why that particular sparrow should fall at that particular moment and in that particular place. I cannot see why all things should not move in a divine and wonderful order, and yet why they should not all work together for good to those who love God. The Psalmist of old finds no contradiction between the two thoughts. Rather does the one of them seem to him to explain the other. 'All things,' says he, 'continue this day as at the beginning. For all things serve Thee.'

Still it is not to be denied, that this question has been a difficult one to men in all ages, and that it is so to many now.

But be that as it may, this I say, that, of all men, seafaring men are the most likely to solve this great puzzle about the limits of science and of religion, of law and of providence; for, of all callings, theirs needs at once most science and most religion; theirs is most subject to laws, and yet most at the mercy of Providence. And I say that many seafaring men have solved the puzzle for themselves in a very rational and sound way, though they may not be able to put thoughts into words; and that they do show, by their daily conduct, that a man may be at once thoroughly scientific and thoroughly religious. And I say that this Ancient and Honourable Corporation of the Trinity House is a proof thereof unto this day; a proof that sound science need not make us neglect sound religion, nor sound religion make us neglect sound science.

No man ought to say that seamen have neglected science. It is the fashion among some to talk of sailors as superstitious. They must know very little about sailors, and must be very blind to broad facts, who speak thus of them as a class. Many sailors, doubtless, are superstitious. But I appeal to every master mariner here, whether the superstitious men are generally the religious and godly men; whether it is not generally the most reckless and profligate men of the crew who are most afraid of sailing on a Friday, and who give way to other silly fancies which I shall not mention in this sacred place. And I appeal, too, to public experience, whether many, I may say most, of those to whom seamanship and sea-science owes most, have not been God-fearing Christian men?

Be sure of this, that if seamen, as a class, had been superstitious, they would never have done for science what they have done. And what they have done, all the world knows. To seamen, and to men connected with the sea, what do we not owe, in geography, hydrography, meteorology, astronomy, natural history? At the present moment, the world owes them large improvements in dynamics, and in the new uses of steam and iron. It may be fairly said that the mariner has done more toward the knowledge of Nature than any other personage in the world, save the physician.

For seamen have been forced, by the nature of their calling, to be scientific men. From the very earliest ages in which the first canoe put out to sea, the mariner has been educated by the most practical of all schoolmasters, namely, danger. He has carried his life in his hand day and night; he has had to battle with the most formidable and the most seemingly capricious of the brute powers of nature; with storms, with ice, with currents, with unknown rocks and shoals, with the vicissitudes of climate, and the terrible and seemingly miraculous diseases which change of climate engenders. He has had to fight Nature; and to conquer her, if he could, by understanding her; by observing facts, and by facing facts. He dared not, like a scholar in his study, indulge in theories and fancies about how things ought to be. He had to find out how they really were. He dared not say, According to my theory of the universe this current ought to run in such a direction; he had to find out which way it did actually run, according to God's method of the universe, lest it should run him ashore. Everywhere, I say, and all day long, the seaman has to observe facts and to use facts, unless he intends to be drowned; and therefore, so far from being a superstitious man, who refuses to inquire into facts, but puts vain dreams in their stead, the sailor is for the most part a very scientific-minded man: observant, patient, accurate, truthful; conquering Nature, as the great saying is, because he obeys her.

But if seamen have been forced to be scientific, they have been equally forced to be religious. They that go down to the sea in ships see both the works of the Lord, and also His wonders in the deep. They see God's works, regular, orderly, the same year by year, voyage by voyage, and tide by tide; and they learn the laws of them, and are so far safe. But they also see God's wonders—

strange, sudden, astonishing dangers, which have, no doubt, their laws, but none which man has found out as yet. Over them they cannot reason and foretell; they can only pray and trust. With all their knowledge, they have still plenty of ignorance; and therefore, with all their science, they have still room for religion. Is there an old man in this church who has sailed the seas for many a year, who does not know that I speak truth? Are there not men here who have had things happen to them, for good and for evil, beyond all calculation? who have had good fortune of which they could only say, The glory be to God, for I had no share therein? or who have been saved, as by miracle, from dangers of which they could only say, It was of the Lord's mercies that we were not swallowed up? who must, if they be honest men, as they are, say with the Psalmist, We cried unto the Lord in our trouble, and he delivered us out of our distress?

And this it is that I said at first, that no men were so fit as seamen to solve the question, where science ends and where religion begins; because no men's calling depends so much on science and reason, and so much, at the same time, on Providence and God's merciful will.

Therefore, when men say, as they will,—If this world is governed by fixed laws, and if we have no right to ask God to alter his laws for our sakes, then what use in prayer? I will answer,—Go to the seaman, and ask him what he thinks. The puzzle may seem very great to a comfortable landsman, sitting safe in his study at home; but it ought to be no puzzle at all to the master mariner in his cabin, with his chart and his Bible open before him, side by side. He ought to know well enough where reason stops and religion begins. He ought to know when to work, and when to pray. He ought to know the laws of the sea and of the sky. But he ought to know too how to pray, without asking God to alter those laws, as presumptuous and superstitious men are wont to do.

Take as an instance the commonest of all —a storm. We know that storms are not caused (as folk believed in old time) by evil spirits; that they are natural phenomena, obeying certain fixed laws; that they are necessary from time to time; that they are probably, on the whole, useful.

And we know two ways of facing a storm, one of which you may see too often among the boatmen of the Mediterranean—How a man shall say, I know nothing as to how, or why, or when, a storm should come; and I care not to know. If one falls on me, I will cry for help to the Panagia, or St. Nicholas, or some other saint, and perhaps they will still the storm by miracle. That is superstition, the child of ignorance and fear.

And you may have seen what comes of that temper of mind. How, when the storm comes, instead of order, you have confusion; instead of courage, cowardice; instead of a calm and manly faith, a miserable crying of every man to his own saint, while the vessel is left to herself to sink or swim.

But what is the temper of true religion, and of true science likewise? The seaman will say, I dare not pray that there may be no storm. I cannot presume to interfere with God's government. If there ought to be a storm, there will be one: if not, there will be none. But I can forecast the signs of the weather; I can consult my barometer; I can judge, by the new lights of science, what course the storm will probably take; and I can do my best to avoid it.

But does that make religion needless? Does that make prayer useless? How so? The seaman may say, I dare not pray that the storm may not come. But there is no necessity that I should be found in its path. And I may pray, and I will pray, that God may so guide and govern my voyage, and all its little accidents, that I may pass it by. I know that I can forecast the storm somewhat; and if I do not try to do that, I am tempting God: but I may pray, I will pray, that my forecast may be correct. I will pray the Spirit of God, who gives man understanding, to give me a right judgment, a sound mind, and a calm heart, that I may make no mistake and neglect no precaution; and if I fail, and sink—God's will be done. It is a good will to me and all my crew; and into the hands of the good God who has redeemed me, I commend my spirit, and their spirits likewise.

This much, therefore, we may say of prayer. We may always pray to be made better men. We may always pray to be made wiser men. These prayers will always be answered; for they are prayers for the very Spirit of God himself, from whom comes all goodness and all wisdom, and it can never be wrong to ask to be made right.

There are surely, too, evils so terrible, that when they threaten us—if God being our Father means anything,—if Christ being our example means anything—then we have a right to cry, like our Lord himself, 'Father, if it be possible, let this cup pass from me:' if we only add, like our Lord, 'Nevertheless, not as I will, but as Thou wilt.'

And of dangers in general this we may say—that if we pray against known dangers which we can avoid, we do nothing but tempt God: but that against unknown and unseen dangers we may always pray. For instance, if a sailor needlessly lodges over a foul, tideless harbour, or sleeps in a tropical mangrove swamp, he has no right to pray against cholera and fever; for he has done his best to give himself cholera and fever, and has thereby tempted God. But if he goes into a new land, of whose climate, diseases, dangers, he is utterly ignorant, then he has surely a right to pray God to deliver him from those dangers; and if not,—if he is doomed to suffer from them,—to pray God that he may discover and understand the new dangers of that new land, in order to warn future travellers against them, and so make his private suffering a benefit to mankind.

This, then, is our duty as to known dangers, —to guard ourselves against them by science, and the reason which God has given us; and as to unknown dangers, to pray to God to deliver us from them, if it seem good to him: but above all, to pray to him to deliver us from them in the best way, the surest way, the most lasting way, the way in which we may not only preserve ourselves, but our fellow-men and generations yet unborn; namely, by giving us wisdom and understanding to discover the dangers, to comprehend them, and to conquer them, by reason and by science.

This is the spirit of sound science and of sound religion. And it was in this spirit, and for this very end, that this Ancient and Honourable Corporation of the Trinity House was founded more than three hundred years ago. Not merely to pray to God and to the saints, after the ancient fashion, to deliver all poor mariners from dangers of the seas. That was a natural prayer, and a pious one, as far as it went: but it did not go far enough. For, as a fact, God did not always answer it: he did not always see fit to deliver those who called upon him. Gallant ships went down with all their crews. It was plain that God would not always deliver poor mariners, even though they cried to him in their distress.

Then, in the sixteenth century, when men's minds were freed from many old superstitions, by a better understanding both of Holy Scripture and of the laws of nature, the master mariners of England took a wiser course.

They said, God will not always help poor mariners: but he will always teach them to deliver themselves. And so they built this House, not in the name of the Virgin Mary or any saints in heaven, but, with a deep understanding of what was needed, in the most awful name of God himself. Thereby they went to the root and ground of this matter, and of all matters. They went to the source of all law and order; to the source of all force and life; and to the source, likewise, of all love and mercy; when they founded their House in the name of the Father of Lights, in whom men live and move and have their being; from whom comes every good and perfect gift, and without whom not a sparrow falls to the ground; in the name of the Son, who was born on earth a man, and tasted sorrow, and trial, and death for every man; in the name of the Holy Ghost, who inspires man with the spirit of wisdom and understanding, and gives him a right judgment in all things, putting into his heart good desires, and enabling him to bring them to good effect. And so, believing that the ever-blessed Trinity would teach them to help themselves and their fellow-mariners, they set to work, like truly God-fearing men, not to hire monks to sing and say masses for them, but to set up for themselves lights and sea-marks, and to take order for the safe navigation of these seas, like men who believed indeed that they were the children of God, and that God would prosper his children in as far as they used that reason which he himself had bestowed upon them.

It is for these men's sakes, as well as for our own, that we are met together here this day. We are met to commemorate the noble dead; not in any Popish or superstitious fashion, as if they needed our prayers, or we needed their miraculous assistance: but in the good old Protestant scriptural sense—to thank God for all his servants departed this life in his faith and fear, and to pray that God may give us grace to follow their good examples; and especially to thank him for the founders of this ancient Trinity House, which stands here as a token to all generations of Britons, that science and religion are not contrary to each other, but twin sisters, meant to aid each other and mankind in the battle with the brute forces of this universe.

We are met together here to thank God for all gallant mariners, and for all who have helped mariners toward safety and success; for all who have made discoveries in hydrography or meteorology, in navigation, or in commerce, adding to the safety of seamen, and to the health and wealth of the human race; for all who have set noble examples to their crews, facing danger manfully and dying at their posts, as many a man has died, a martyr to his duty; for all who, living active, and useful, and virtuous lives in their sea calling, have ended as they lived, God-fearing Christian men.

To thank God for all these we are met together here; and to pray to God likewise that he would send his Spirit into the hearts of seamen, and of those who deal with seamen; and specially into the hearts of the Royal the Master and the Worshipful the Elder Brethren of this Ancient and Honourable House; that they may be true, and loyal, and obedient to that divine name in which they are met together here this day—the name of Father, Son, and Holy Ghost, the ever-blessed Trinity, the giver of all good gifts, in whom we live, and move, and have our being; always keeping God's commandments and looking for God's guidance, and setting to those beneath them an example of sound reason, virtue, and religion; that so there may never be wanting to this land a race of seamen who shall trust in God to teach them all they need to know, and to dispose of their bodies and souls as seemeth best to his most holy will; who, fearing God, shall fear nought else, but shall defy the dangers of the seas, and all the brute forces of climates and of storms; who shall set in foreign lands an example of justice and mercy, of true civilization and true religion; and so shall still maintain the marine of Great Britain, as it has been for now three hundred years, a safeguard and a glory to these islands, and a blessing to the coasts of all the world.

SERMON IV.

GOD'S TRAINING.

DEUTERONOMY VIII. 2—5.

And thou shalt remember all the way which the Lord thy God led thee these forty years in the wilderness, to humble thee, and to prove thee, to know what was in thine heart, whether thou wouldest keep his commandments or no. And he humbled thee, and suffered thee to hunger, and fed thee with manna, which thou knewest not, neither did thy fathers know; that he might make thee know that man doth not live by bread only, but by every word that proceedeth out of the mouth of the Lord doth man live. Thy raiment waxed not old upon thee, neither did thy foot swell, these forty years. Thou shalt also consider in thine heart, that, as a man chasteneth his son, so the Lord thy God chasteneth thee.

THIS is the lesson of our lives. This is God's training, not only for the old Jews, but for us. What was true of them, is more or less true of us. And we read these verses to teach us that God's ways with man do not change; that his fatherly hand is over us, as well as over the people of Israel; that we are in God's schoolhouse, as they were; that their blessings are our blessings, their dangers are our dangers; that, as St. Paul says, all these things are written for our example.

'And he humbled thee, and suffered thee to hunger.' How true to life that is! How often there comes to a man, at his setting out in life, a time which humbles him; a time of disappointment, when he finds that he is not so clever as he thought, as able to help himself as he thought; when his fine plans fail him; when he does not know how to settle in life, how to marry, how to provide for a family. Perhaps the man actually does hunger, and go through a time of want and struggle. Then, it may be, he cries in his heart—How hard it is for me! How hard that the golden days of youth should be all dark and clouded over! How hard to have to suffer anxiety and weary hard work, just when I am able to enjoy myself most!

It is hard: but worse things than hard things may happen to a man. Far worse is it to grow up, as some men do, in wealth, and ease, and luxury, with all the pleasures of this life found ready to their hands. Some men, says the proverb, are 'born with a golden spoon in their mouth.' God help them if they are! Idleness, profligacy, luxury, self-conceit, no care for their duty, no care for God, no feeling that they are in God's school-house— these are too often the fruits of that breeding up. How hardly will they learn that man doth not live by bread alone, or by money alone, or by comfort alone, but by every word that proceedeth out of the mouth of God. Truly, said our Lord, 'how hardly shall they ‘that have riches enter into the kingdom of ‘heaven.' Not those who earn riches by manful and honest labour; not those who come to wealth after long training to make them fit to use wealth: but those who have wealth; who are born amid luxury and pomp; who have never known want, and the golden lessons which want brings.—God help them, for they need his help even more than the poor young man who is at his wit's end how to live. For him God is helping. His very want, and struggles, and anxiety may be God's help to him. They help him to control himself, and do with a little; they help him to strengthen his character, and to bring out all the powers of mind that God has given him. God is humbling him, that he may know that man doth not live by bread alone, but by every word which proceedeth out of the mouth of God. God, too, if he trusts in God, will feed him with manna— spiritual manna, not bodily. He fed the Jews in the wilderness with manna, to show them that his power was indeed almighty—that if he did not see fit to help his people in one way, he could help them just as easily in another. And so with every man who trusts in God. In unforeseen ways, he is helped. In unforeseen ways, he prospers; his life, as he goes on, becomes very different from what he expected, from what he would have liked; his fine dreams fade away, as he finds the world quite another place from what he fancied it: but still he prospers. If he be earnest and honest, patient and God-fearing, he prospers; God brings him through. His raiment doth not wax old, neither doth his foot swell, through all his forty years' wandering in the wilderness. He is not tired out, he does not break down, though he may have to work long and hard. As his day is, so his strength shall be. God holds him up, strengthens and refreshes him, and brings him through years of labour from the thought of which he shrank when he was young.

And so the man learns that man doth not live by bread alone, but by every word that proceedeth out of the mouth of God; that not in the abundance of things which he possesses, not in money; not in pleasure, not even in comforts, does the life of man consist: but in this—to learn his duty, and to have strength from God to do it. Truly said the prophet—'It is good for a man to learn to bear the yoke in his youth.'

After that sharp training a man will prosper; because he is fit to prosper. He has learnt the golden lesson. He can be trusted with comforts, wealth, honour. Let him have them, if God so will, and use them well.

Only, only, when a time of ease and peace

comes to him in his middle age, let him not forget the warning of the latter part of the chapter.

For there is another danger awaiting him, as it awaited those old Jews; the danger of prosperity in old age. Ah my friends, that is a sore temptation—the sorest, perhaps, which can meet a man in the long struggle of life, the temptation which success brings. In middle age, when he has learnt his business, and succeeded in it; when he has fought his battle with the world, and conquered more or less; when he has made his way up, and seems to himself safe, and comfortable, and thriving; when he feels that he is a shrewd, thrifty, experienced man, who knows the world and how to prosper in it—Then how easy it is for him to say in his heart—as Moses feared that those old Jews would say—'My might and 'the power of my wit has gotten me this 'wealth,' and to forget the Lord his God, who guided him and trained him through all the struggles and storms of early life; and so to become vainly confident, worldly and hard-hearted, undevout and ungodly, even though he may keep himself respectable enough, and fall into no open sin.

Therefore it is, I think, that while we see so many lives which have been sad lives of poverty, and labour, and struggle, end peacefully and cheerfully, in a sunshiny old age, like a still bright evening after a day of storm and rain; so on the other hand we see lives which have been prosperous and happy ones for many years, end sadly in bereavement, poverty, or disappointment, as did the life of David, the man after God's own heart. God guided him through all the dangers and temptations of youth, and through them all he trusted God. God brought him safely to success, honour, a royal crown; and he thanked God, and acknowledged his goodness. And yet after a while his heart was puffed up, and he forgot God, and all he owed to God, and became a tyrant, an adulterer, a murderer. He repented of his sin: but he could not escape the punishment of it. His children were a curse to him; the sword never departed from his house; and his last years were sad enough, and too sad.

Perhaps that was God's mercy to him; God's way of remembering him again, and bringing him back to him. Perhaps too that same is God's way of bringing back many a man in our own days who has wandered from him in success and prosperity.

God grant that we may never need that terrible chastisement. God grant that we, if success and comfort come to us, may never wander so far from God, but that we may be brought back to him by the mere humbling of old age itself, without needing affliction over and above.

Yes, by old age alone. Old age, it seems to me, is a most wholesome and blessed medicine for the soul of man. Good it is to find that we can work no longer, and rejoice no more in our own strength and cunning. Good it is to feel our mortal bodies decay, and to learn that we are but dust, and that when we turn again to our dust, all our thoughts will perish. Good it is to see the world changing round us, going ahead of us, leaving us and our opinions behind. Good perhaps for us— though not for them—to see the young who are growing up around us looking down on our old-fashioned notions. Good for us: because anything is good which humbles us, makes us feel our own ignorance, weakness, nothingness, and cast ourselves utterly on that God in whom we live, and move, and have our being; and on the mercy of that Saviour who died for us on the Cross; and on that Spirit of God from whose holy inspiration alone all good desires and good actions come.

God grant that that may be our end. That old age, when it comes, may chasten us, humble us, soften us; and that our second childhood may be a second childhood indeed, purged from the conceit, the scheming, the fierceness, the covetousness which so easily beset us in our youth and manhood; and tempered down to gentleness, patience, humility, and faith. God grant that instead of clinging greedily to life, and money, and power, and fame, we may cling only to God, and have one only wish as we draw near our end.—'From my youth up hast thou taught 'me, Oh God, and hitherto I have declared 'thy wondrous works. Now also that I am 'old and grey-headed, Oh Lord, forsake me 'not, till I have showed thy goodness to this 'generation, and thy power to those who are 'yet to come.'

SERMON V.

GOOD FRIDAY.

HEBREWS IX. 13, 14.

For if the blood of bulls and of goats, and the ashes of an heifer sprinkling the unclean, sanctifieth to the purifying of the flesh: How much more shall the blood of Christ, who through the eternal Spirit offered himself without spot to God, purge your conscience from dead works to serve the living God?

THE three collects for Good Friday are very grand and very remarkable. In the first we pray:—

'Almighty God, we beseech thee graciously
'to behold this thy family, for which our Lord
'Jesus Christ was contented to be betrayed,
'and given up into the hands of wicked men,
'and to suffer death upon the cross, who now
'liveth and reigneth with thee and the Holy
'Ghost ever one God, world without end.
'Amen.'

In the second we pray :—

'Almighty and everlasting God, by whose
'Spirit the whole body of the Church is go-
'verned and sanctified : Receive our supplica-
'tions and prayers, which we offer before
'thee for all estates of men in thy holy
'Church, that every member of the same, in
'his vocation and ministry, may truly and
'godly serve thee; through our Lord and
'Saviour Jesus Christ. Amen.'

In the third we pray :—

'O merciful God, who hast made all men,
'and hatest nothing that thou hast made, nor
'wouldest the death of a sinner, but rather
'that he should be converted and live : Have
'mercy upon all Jews, Turks, Infidels, and
'Hereticks, and take from them all ignorance,
'hardness of heart, and contempt of thy
'Word; and so fetch them home, blessed
'Lord, to thy flock, that they may be saved
'among the remnant of the true Israelites,
'and be made one fold under one shepherd,
'Jesus Christ our Lord, who liveth and reign-
'eth with thee and the Holy Spirit, one God,
'world without end. Amen.'

Now these collects give us the keynote of Good Friday; they tell us what the Church wishes us to think of on Good Friday.

We are to think of Christ's death and passion. Of that there is no doubt.

But we need not on Good Friday, or perhaps at any other time, trouble our minds with the unfathomable questions, How did Christ's sacrifice take away our sins? How does Christ's blood purge our conscience?

Mere 'theories of the Atonement,' as they are called, have very little teaching in them, and still less comfort. Wise and good men have tried their minds upon them in all ages; they have done their best to explain Christ's sacrifice, and the atonement which he worked out on the cross on Good Friday: but it does not seem to me that they have succeeded. I never read yet any explanation which I could fully understand; which fully satisfied my conscience, or my reason either; or which seemed to me fully to agree with and explain all the texts of Scripture bearing on this great subject.

But is it possible to explain the matter?

Is it not too deep for mortal man? Is it not one of the deep things of God, and of God alone, before which we must worship and believe? As for explaining or understanding it, must not that be impossible, from its very nature?

For, consider the first root and beginning of the whole question. Put it in the simplest shape, to which all Christians will agree. The Father sent the Son to die for the world. Most true: but who can explain those words? We are stopped at the very first step by an abyss. Who can tell us what is meant by the Father sending the Son? What is the relation, the connexion, between the Father and the Son? If we do not know that, we can know nothing about the matter, about the very root and ground thereof. And we do know little or nothing. The Bible only gives us scattered hints here and there. It is one of the things of which we may say, with St. Paul, that we know in part, and see through a glass darkly. How, then, dare we talk as if we knew all, as if we saw clearly? The atonement is a blessed and awful mystery hidden in God: ordained by and between God the Father and God the Son. And who can search out that? Who hath known the mind of the Lord, or who hath been his counsellor? Did we sit by, and were we taken into his counsels, when he made the world? Not we. Neither were we when he redeemed the world. He did it. Let that be enough for us. And he did it in love. Let that be enough for us.

God the Father so loved the world, that he sent his Son into the world, that the world by him might be saved. God the Son so loved the world, that he came to do his Father's will, and put away sin by the sacrifice of himself. That is enough for us. Let it be enough; and let us take simply, honestly, literally, and humbly, like little children, everything which the Bible says about it, without trying or pretending to understand, but only to believe.

We can believe that Christ's blood can purge our conscience, though we cannot explain in any words of our own how it can do so. We can believe that God made him to be sin for us, who knew no sin, though we not only cannot but dare not try to explain so awful a mystery. We can believe that Christ's sacrifice on the cross was a propitiation for sin, though neither we, nor (as I hold) any man on earth, can tell exactly what the words sacrifice and propitiation mean. And so with all the texts which speak of Christ's death and passion, and that atonement for sin which he, in his boundless mercy, worked out this day. Let us not torment our minds with arguments in which there are a hundred words of man's invention to one word of Holy Scripture, while the one word of Scripture has more in it than the hundred words of man can explain. But let us have faith in Christ. I mean, let us trust him that he has done all that can or need be done; that whatsoever was needed to reconcile God to man, he has done, for he is perfect God; that whatever was needed to reconcile man to God, he has done, for he is perfect man.

Let us, instead of puzzling ourselves as to how the Lamb of God takes away the sins of the world, believe that he knows, and that he lives, and cry to him as to the living God,—

Lamb of God, who takest away the sins of the world, have mercy on us, and take our sins away.

And let us beseech God this day, graciously to behold his family, the nations of Christendom, for which our Lord Jesus Christ was contented to be betrayed into the hands of wicked men, and suffer death upon the cross. Let us ask this, even though we do not fully understand what Christ's death on the cross did for mankind. That was the humble, childlike, really believing spirit of the early Christians. God grant us the same spirit; we need it much in these very times.

For if we are of that spirit, my friends, then, instead of tormenting our minds as to the how and why of Christ's sacrifice on the cross, we shall turn our hearts, and not merely our minds, to the practical question—What shall we do? If Christ died for us, what shall we do? What shall we ask God to help us to do? To that the second collect gives a clear answer at once—Serve the living God.

And how? By dead works? By mere outward forms and ceremonies, church-goings, psalm-singings, sermon-hearings? Not so. These are right and good; but they are dead works, which cannot take away sin, any more than could the gifts and sacrifices, the meats and drinks of the old Jewish law. Those, says St. Paul, could not make him that did the sacrifice perfect as pertaining to the conscience. They could not give him a clear conscience; they could not make him sure that God had forgiven him; they could not give him spirit and comfort to say—Now I can leave the church a forgiven man, a new man, and begin a fresh life; and go about my daily business in joyfulness and peace of mind, sure that God will help me, and bless me, and enable me to serve him in my calling.

No, says St. Paul. More than dead works are wanted to purge a man's conscience. Nothing will do that but the blood of Christ. And that will do it. He, the spotless Lamb, has offered himself to God, as a full and perfect and sufficient sacrifice, offering, and satisfaction for the sins of the whole world; and therefore for thy sins, whoever thou art, be thy sins many or few. Believe that; for thou art a man for whom Christ died. Claim thy share in Christ's blood. Believe that he has died for thee; that he has blotted out thy sins in the blood of his cross; that thou needest not try to blot them out by any dead works, forms, or ceremonies whatsoever; for Christ has done and suffered already all for thee. Thou art forgiven. Put away thy sins, for God has put them away; rise, and be a new man. Thou art one of God's holy Church. God has justified thee. Let him sanctify thee likewise. God's spirit is with thee to guide thee, to inspire thee, and make thee holy. Serve thy Father and thy Master, the Living God, sure that he is satisfied with thee for Christ's sake; that thou art in thy right state henceforward; in thy right place in this world; and that he blesses all thy efforts to live a right life, and to do thy duty.

But how to serve him, and where? By doing something strange and fantastic? By giving up thy business, money, time? Going to the ends of the earth? Making what some will call some great sacrifice for God?

Not so. All that may be, and generally

is, the fruit of mere self-will and self-conceit. God has made a sacrifice for thee. Let that be enough. If he wants thee to make a sacrifice to him in return, he will compel thee to make it, doubt it not. But meanwhile abide in the calling wherein thou art called. Do the duty which lies nearest thee. Whether thou art squire or labourer, rich or poor; whether thy duty is to see after thy children, or to mind thy shop, do thy duty. For that is thy vocation and calling; that is the ministry in which thou canst serve God, by serving thy fellow-creatures for whom Christ died.

This day the grand prayer has gone up throughout Christ's Church—and thou hast joined in it—for all estates of men in his holy Church; for all estates, from kings and statesmen governing the nations, down to labouring men tilling in the field, and poor women washing and dressing their children at home, that each and all of them may do their work well, whatever it is, and thereby serve the Living God. For now their work, however humble, is God's work; Christ has bought it and redeemed it with his blood. When he redeemed human nature, he redeemed all that human nature can and ought to do, save sin. All human duties and occupations are purified by the blood of Christ's cross; and if we do our duty well, we do it to the Lord, and not to man; and the Lord blesses us therein, and will help us to fulfil our work like Christian men, by the help of his Holy Spirit.

And for those who know not Christ? For them, too, we can pray. For, for them too Christ died. They, too, belong to Christ, for he has bought them with his most precious blood. What will happen to them we know not: but this we know, that they are his sheep, lost sheep though they may be; and that we are bound to pray, that he would bring them home to his flock.

But how will he bring them back? That, again, we know not. But why need we know? If Christ knows how to do it, surely we need not. Let us trust him to do his own work in his own way.

But will he do it? My friends, if we wish for the salvation of all Jews, Turks, Infidels, and Heretics, do you suppose that we are more compassionate to them than God who made them? Who is more likely to pity the heathen? We who send a few missionaries to teach them: or God who sent his own Son to die for them?

Oh trust God, and trust Christ; for this, as for all other things. Believe that for the heathen, as for us, he is able to do exceedingly and abundantly beyond all that we can ask or think; and believe too, that if we do ask, we do not ask in vain; that this collect which has gone up every Good Friday for centuries past, from millions of holy hearts throughout the world, has not gone up unheard; that it will be answered—we know not how—but answered still; and that to Jew and Turk, Heathen and Heretic, this day will prove hereafter to have been, what it is to us, Good Friday.

SERMON VI.

FALSE CIVILIZATION.

JEREMIAH XXXV. 19.

Thus saith the Lord of hosts, the God of Israel; Jonadab the son of Rechab shall not want a man to stand before me for ever.

LET us think a while this morning what this text has to do with us; and why this strange story of the Rechabites is written for our instruction, in the pages of Holy Scripture.

Let us take the story as it stands, and search the Scriptures simply for it. For the Bible will surely tell its own story best, and teach its own lesson best.

These Rechabites, who were they? Or, indeed we may ask—Who are they? For they are said to exist still.

They were not Israelites, but wild Arabs, a branch of the Kenite tribe, which claimed

—at least its chiefs—to be descended from Abraham, by his wife Keturah. They joined the Israelites, and wandered with them into the land of Canaan. But they never settled down, as the Israelites did, into farmers and townsfolk. They never became what we call civilized: though they had a civilization of their own, which stood them in good stead, and kept them—and keeps them, it would seem, to this day,—strong and prosperous, while great cities and mighty nations have been destroyed round about them. They kept their old simple Arab customs, living in their great black camels' hair tents, feeding their flocks and herds, as they wandered from forest to forest and lawn to lawn, living on the milk of the flock, and it would seem, on locusts and wild honey, as did John the Baptist after them. They had (as many Arab tribes have still) neither corn, seed-field, nor vineyard. Wild men they were in their ways, yet living a simple wholesome life; till in the days of Ahab and Jehu there arose among them a chief called Jonadab the son of Rechab, of the house of Hammath. Why he was called the son of Rechab is not clearly known. 'The son of the rider,' or 'the son of the chariot,' seems to be the most probable meaning of the name. So that these Rechabites, at least, had horses—as many Arab tribes have now —and whether they rode them, or used them to draw their goods about in carts, like many other wild tribes, they seem to have gained from Jonadab the name of Rechabim, the sons of Rechab, the sons of the rider, or the sons of the chariot.

Of Jonadab the son of Rechab, you heard three Sundays since, in that noble passage of 2 Kings x. where Jehu, returning from the slaughter of the idolatrous kings, and going to slay the priests of Baal, meets Jonadab and asks him, Is thy heart right—that is, sound in the worship of God, and determined to put down idolatry—as my heart is with thy heart? We hear of him and his tribe no more till the days of Jeremiah, 250 years after, in the story from which my text is taken. What Jonadab's reasons may have been for commanding his tribe neither to settle in towns, nor till the ground, it is not difficult to guess. He may have dreaded lest his people, by settling in the towns, should learn the idolatry of the Israelites. He may have dreaded, likewise, lest they should give way to that same luxury and profligacy in which the Israelites indulged—and especially lest they should be demoralized by that drunkenness of which the prophets speak, as one of the crying sins of that age. He may have feared, too, lest their settling down as landholders or townsmen would cause them to be absorbed and lost among the nation of the Israelites, and probably involved in their ruin. Be that as it may, he laid his command upon his tribe, and his command was obeyed.

Of the after-history of these simple God-fearing folk we know very little. But what we do know is well worth remembering. They were, it seems, carried away captive to Babylon with the rest of the Jews; and with them they came back to Jerusalem. Meanwhile, they had intermarried with the priests of the tribe of Levi; and they assisted at the worship and sacrifices,—'standing before the Lord' (as Jeremiah had foretold) 'in the temple,' but living (as some say) outside the walls in their tents. And it is worth remembering, that we have one psalm in the Bible, which was probably written either by one of these Rechabites, or by Jeremiah for them to sing, and that a psalm which you all know well, the old man's psalm, as it has well been called—the 71st Psalm, which is read in the visitation of the sick; which says, 'O God, 'thou hast taught me from my youth: and 'hitherto have I declared thy wondrous works. 'Now also when I am old and grey-headed, 'O God, forsake me not; until I have shewed 'thy strength unto this generation, and thy 'power to every one that is to come.'

It was, moreover, a Rechabite priest, we are told—'one of the sons of the Rechabim 'spoken of by Jeremiah the prophet'—who when the Jews were stoning St. James the Just, one of the twelve apostles, cried out against their wickedness.

What befell the Rechabites when Jerusalem was destroyed, we know not: but they seem to have returned to their old life, and wandered away into the far east; for in the twelfth century, more than one thousand years after, a Jewish traveller met with them 100,000 strong under a Jewish prince of the house of David; still abstaining from wine and flesh, and paying tithes to teachers who studied the law, and wept for the fall of Jerusalem. And even yet they are said to endure and prosper. For in our own time, a traveller met the Rechabites once more in the heart of Arabia, still living in their tents, still calling themselves the sons of Jonadab. With one of them, Mousa (*i.e.* Moses) by name, he talked, and Mousa said to him, 'Come, and I will show you who we are;' and from an Arabic bible he read the words of my text, and said, ' You will find us 60,000 in number still. ' See, the words of the prophet have been ful- ' filled—" Jonadab the son of Rechab shall ' not want a man to stand before me for ' ever."'

What lesson shall we learn from this story —so strange, and yet so beautiful? What lesson need we learn, save that which the Holy

Scripture itself bids us learn? The blessing which comes upon reverence for our forefathers, and above all for God, our Father in Heaven.

Reverence for our forefathers. These are days in which we are too apt to sneer at those who have gone before us; to look back on our forefathers as very ignorant, prejudiced, old-fashioned people, whose opinions have been all set aside by the progress of knowledge.

Be sure that in this temper of mind lies a sin and a snare. If we wish to keep up true independence and true self-respect in ourselves and our children, we should be careful to keep up respect for our forefathers. A shallow, sneering generation, which laughs at those who have gone before it, is ripe for disaster and slavery. We are not bound, of course—as those old Rechabites considered themselves bound—to do in everything exactly what our forefathers did. For we are not under the law, but under grace; and where the Spirit of the Lord is, there is liberty— liberty to change, improve, and develop as the world grows older, and (we may hope) wiser. But we are bound to do, not exactly what our forefathers did, but what we may reasonably suppose that they would have done, had they lived now, and were they in our places. We are to obey them, not in the letter, but in the spirit.

And whenever, in the prayer for the Church militant, we commemorate the faithful dead, and thank God for all his servants departed this life in his faith and fear, we should remember with honest pride that we are thanking God for our own mothers and fathers, and for those that went before them; ay, for every honest God-fearing man and woman, high or low, who ever did their duty by God and their neighbours, and left, when they died, a spot of this land somewhat better than they found it.

And for God; the Father of all fathers; our Father in heaven—Oh, my friends, God grant that it may never be said to any of us, Behold the words of Jonadab the son of Rechab, which he commanded his children, are performed: but ye have not hearkened unto me. I have sent also unto you, saith God, not merely my servants the prophets, but my only-begotten, Jesus Christ your Lord, saying, 'Return you now every man from his evil 'way, and amend your doings, and go not after 'other gods to serve them, and ye shall dwell 'in the land which I have given to you and to 'your fathers. But ye have not inclined your 'ear, nor hearkened unto me.'

God grant that that may never be said to any of us. And yet it is impossible to deny —impossible to shut our eyes to the plain fact—that Englishmen now-a-days are more and more forgetting that there are any commandments of God whatsoever; any everlasting laws laid down by their Heavenly Father, which, if they break, will avenge themselves by our utter ruin. We do not go after other gods, it is true, in the sense of worshipping idols. But there is another god, which we go after more and more; and that is money; gain; our interest (as we call it):—not knowing that the only true interest of any man is to fear God and keep his commandments. We hold more and more that a man can serve God and mammon; that a man must of course be religious, and belong to some special sect, or party, or denomination, and stand up for that fiercely enough : but we do not hold that there are commandments of God which say for ever to the sinner, 'Do this and thou shalt live;' 'Do this or thou shalt die.'

We hold that because we are not under the law, but under grace, there is no condemnation for sin—at least for the special sort of sin which happens to be in fashion, which is now-a-days the sin of making money at all risks. We hold that there is one law of morality for the kingdom of heaven, and another for the kingdom of mammon. Therefore we hold, more and more, that when money is in question anything and everything is fair. There are—we have reason to know it just now but too well—thousands who will sell their honour, their honesty, yea, their own souls, for a few paltry pounds, and think no shame. And if any one says, with Jeremiah the prophet, ' These are poor, they know not the way ' of the Lord, nor the judgment of their God. ' I will get me to the great men, for they have ' known the way of the Lord, and the judg- ' ment of their God :'—then will he find, as

Jeremiah did, that too many of these great and wealthy worshippers of mammon have utterly broken the yoke, and burst the bonds, of all moral law of right and wrong: heaping up vast fortunes amid the ruin of those who have trusted them, and the tears of the widow and the orphan, by means now glossed over by fine new words, but called in plain honest old English by a very ugly name.

How many there are in England now, my friends, who would laugh in their hearts at those worthy Rechabites, and hold them to be ignorant, old-fashioned, bigoted people, for keeping up their poor, simple, temperate life, wandering to and fro with their tents and cattle, instead of dwelling in great cities, and making money, and becoming what is now-a-days called civilized, in luxury and covetousness. Surely according to the wisdom of this world, the Rechabites were foolish enough. But it is the wisdom of this world itself— not simplicity and loyalty like theirs—which is foolishness with God.

My friends, let us all take warning, each man for himself. When a nation corrupts itself—as we seem inclined to do now, by luxury and covetousness, selfishness and self-will, forgetting more and more loyalty and order, honesty and high principle—then some wholesome, but severe judgment of God, is sure to come upon that nation: a day in which all faces shall gather blackness: a day of gloominess and thick darkness, like the morning spread upon the mountains.

For the eternal laws of God's providence are still at work, though we choose to forget them; and the Judge who administers them is the same yesterday, to-day, and for ever, even Jesus Christ the Lord, the everlasting Rock, on which all morality and all society is founded. Whosoever shall fall on that Rock in repentance and humility, confessing, bewailing, and forsaking his worldliness and sinfulness, he shall indeed be broken: but of him it is written, 'The sacrifices of 'God are a broken spirit: a broken and a 'contrite heart, O God, thou wilt not despise.' And he shall find that Rock, even Christ, a safe standing-ground amid the slippery mire of this world's temptations, and the storms and floods of trouble which are coming—it may be in our children's days—it may be in our own.

But he who hardens his heart: he who says proudly, 'We are they that ought to speak; who is Lord over us?'—he who says carelessly, 'Soul, take thine ease; thou hast much goods laid up for many years'—he who halts between two opinions, and believes to the last that he can serve both God and mammon—he, especially, who fancies that falsehood, injustice, covetousness, and neglect of his fellow-men, can properly be his interest, or help his interest in any wise—of all such it is written, 'On whomsoever that Rock'—even the eternal laws of Christ the Judge—' On ' whomsoever that Rock shall fall, it shall ' grind him to powder.'

SERMON VII.

THE NAME OF GOD.

Isaiah L. 10.

Who is among you that feareth the Lord, that obeyeth the voice of his servant, that walketh in darkness, and hath no light? Let him trust in the name of the Lord, and stay upon his God.

TO some persons it may seem strange advice to tell them, that in the hour of darkness, doubt, and sorrow, they will find no comfort like that of meditating on the Name of the Ever-blessed Trinity. Yet there is not a prophet or psalmist of the Old Testament who does not speak of 'The Name of the Lord,' as a kind of talisman against all the troubles which can befall the spirit of man. And we, as Christians, know, or ought to know, far more of God than did even prophets or psalmists. If they found comfort in the name of God, we ought to find far more.

But some will say—Yes. Let us think of God, God's mercies, God's dealings with his people; but why think especially of the Name of the Ever-blessed Trinity?

For this simple reason. That it is by that Name of Father, Son, and Holy Ghost, that God has revealed himself. That is the name by which he bids us think of him; and we are more or less disregarding his commands when we think of him by any other. That is the name which God has given himself; and, therefore, it is morally certain that that is God's right name; that it expresses God's very self, God's very being, as he is.

Theology signifies, the knowledge of God as he is. And it is dying out among us in these days. Much of what is called theology now is nothing but experimental religion; which is most important and useful when it is founded on the right knowledge of God: but which is not itself theology. For theology begins with God: but experimental religion, right or wrong, begins with a man's own soul.

Therefore it is that men are unaccustomed to theology. They shrink from it as something very abstruse, only fit for great scholars and divines, and almost given up now-a-days even by them. They do not know that theology, the knowledge of God, is full of practical every-day comfort, and guidance for their conduct and character; yea, that it is—so says the Bible—everlasting life itself. Therefore it is that some shrink from thinking of the Ever-blessed Trinity, not from any evil intent, but because they are afraid of thinking wrongly, and so consider it more safe not to think at all. They have been puzzled, it may be, by arguments which they have heard, or read, or which have risen up in their own minds, and which have made them doubt about the Trinity: and they say—I will not torment my soul, and perhaps endanger my soul, by doubts. I will take the doctrine of the Trinity for granted, because I am bidden to do so: but I leave what it means to be explained by wiser men. If I begin thinking about it I shall only confuse myself. So it is better for me not to think at all.

And one cannot deny that they are right, as far as they go. If they cannot think about the Trinity without thinking wrongly, it is better to take on trust what they are told about it. But they lose much by so doing. They lose the solid and real comfort which they may get by thinking of the Name of God. And, I believe, they lose it unnecessarily. I cannot see why they must think wrongly of the Trinity, if they think at all. I cannot see why they need confuse themselves. The doctrine of the Trinity is not really an unreasonable one. The doubts which come into men's minds concerning it do not seem to me sound and reasonable doubts. For instance, some say—How can there be three persons in one God? It is contrary to reason. One cannot be many. Three cannot be one. That is unreasonable.

I think, that if you will use your reason for yourselves, you will see that it is those words which are unreasonable, and not the doctrine of the Trinity.

First. A thing need not be unreasonable —that is, contrary to reason—because it is above and beyond reason—or, at least, beyond our human reason, which at best (as St. Paul says) sees as in a glass darkly, and only knows in part.

Consider how many things are beyond reason which are not contrary to it. I say that all things which God has made are so: but, without going so far, let us consider these simple examples.

Is it not beyond all reason that among animals, like should bring forth like? Why does an eagle's egg always produce an eagle, and a dove's egg a dove, and so forth? No man knows, no man can give any reason whatsoever. If a dove's egg produced an eagle, ignorant men would cry out at the wonder, the miracle. Wise men know that the real wonder, the real miracle is, that a dove's egg always produces a dove, and not any and every other bird.

Here is a common and notorious fact, entirely above our reason. There is no cause to be given for it, save that God has ordained it so. But it is not contrary to our reason. So far from it, we are certain that a dove will produce a dove; and our reason has found out much of the laws of kind; and found out that they are reasonable laws, regular, and to be depended upon; so that we can, as all know, produce and keep up new breeds whether of plants or of animals.

So that the law of kind, though it is beyond our reason, is not contrary to our reason at all.

So much for things which have life. Take an equally notorious example from things which have not life.

Is it not above and beyond all our reason that the seemingly weakest thing in the world, the most soft and yielding, the most frail and vanishing, should be also one of the strongest things in the world? That is so utterly above reason, that while I say it, it seems to some of you to be contrary to reason, to be unreasonable and impossible. It is so above reason, that till two hundred years ago, no one suspected that it was true. And yet it is strictly true.

What is more soft and yielding, more frail and vanishing, than steam? And what is stronger than steam? I know nothing. Steam it is which has lifted up the mountains from the sea into the clouds. Steam it is which tears to pieces the bowels of the earth with earthquakes and volcanoes, shaking down cities, rasping the solid rocks into powder, and scattering them far and wide in dust over the face of the land.

What gives to steam its enormous force is beyond our reason. We do not know. But so far from being contrary to our reason, we have learnt that the laws of steam are as reasonable as any other of God's laws. We can calculate its force, we can make it, use it, and turn its mighty powers, by reason and science, into our most useful and obedient slave, till it works ten thousand mills, and sends ten thousand ships across the sea.

Above reason, I say, but not contrary to reason, is the mighty power of steam.

And God, who made all these wonders—and millions of wonders more—must he not be more wonderful than them all? Must not his being and essence be above our reason?

But need they be, therefore, contrary to our reason? Not so.

Nevertheless, some will say, How can one be many? How can one be three? Why not? Two are one in you, and every man. Your body is you, and your soul is you. They are two. But you know yourself that you are one being; that the Athanasian Creed speaks, at least, reason when it says, 'As the reasonable soul and the flesh are one 'man, so God and man is one Christ.'

And three are one in every plant in the field. Root, bark, leaves, are three. And yet they are one tree; and if you take away any one of them, the tree will die. So it is in all nature. But why do I talk of a tree, or any other example? Wherever you look you find that one thing is many things, and many things one. So far from that fact being contrary to our reason, it is one which our reason (as soon as we think deeply about this world) assures us is most common. Of every 'organized body' it is strictly true, that it is many things, bound together by a certain law, which makes them one thing and no more. And, therefore, every organized body is a mystery, and above reason: but its organization is none the less true for that.

And there are philosophers who will tell you—and wisely and well—that there must needs be some such mystery in God; that reason ought to teach us—even if revelation had not—two things. First, that God must be one; and next, that God must be many—that is, more than one.

Do I mean that our own reason would have found out for itself the mystery of the ever-blessed Trinity? God forbid! Nothing less.

There surely is a difference between knowing that a thing must be, and knowing that the thing is, and what it is like; and there surely is a difference between knowing that there is a great mystery and wonder in God, and knowing what that mystery is.

Man might have found out that God was one, and yet more than one; but could he have found out what is the essence and character of God? Not his own reason, but the Spirit of God it is which tells him that: tells him that God is Three in One—that these three are persons—that these persons are, a Father, a Son, and a Holy Spirit.

This is what God has himself condescended to tell us; and therefore this is what he specially wishes us to believe and remember when we think of him. This is God's name for himself—Father, Son, and Holy Ghost. Man may give God what name he chooses. God's own name, which he has given himself, is likely surely to be the most correct: at least, it is the one of which God means us to think; for it is the one into which he commanded us to be baptized. Remember that, whenever you hear discourse concerning God; and if any man, however learned, says that God is absolute, answer—'It may be so: but I was not baptized into the name of the absolute.' If he tell you, God is infinite, answer—'It may be so: but I was not baptized into the name of the infinite.' If he tell you, God is the first cause, answer—'That I doubt not: but I was not baptized into the name of the first cause. I was baptized into the name which God has given himself—Father, Son,

'and Holy Ghost; and I will give him no
'other name, and think of him by no other
'name, lest I be committing an act of irreve-
'rence toward God, by presuming to call him
'one thing, when he has bid me call him
'another. Absolute, infinite, first cause, and
'so forth, are deep words: but they are
  words of man's invention, and words too
'which plain, hard-working, hard-sorrowing
'folks do not understand; even if learned
'men do—which I doubt very much indeed:
'and therefore I do not trust them, cannot
'find comfort for my soul in them. But
'Father, Son, and Holy Spirit are words
'which plain, hard-working, hard-sorrowing
'men can understand, and can trust, and can
'find comfort in them; for they are God's own
'words, and, like all God's words, go straight
'home to the hearts of men—straight home
'to the heart of every one who is a father or
'mother—to the heart of every one who has
'a parent or a child—to the heart of every
'one who has the Holy Spirit of God putting
'into his mind good desires, and striving to
'make him bring them into good effect, and

'be, what he knows he should be, a holy and
'good man.'

Answer thus, my friends. And think thus of the mystery of the Ever-blessed Trinity. For this is a thoroughly reasonable plan of thought: and more—in thinking thus you will find comfort, guidance, clearness of head, and clearness of conscience also. Only remember what you are to think of. You are not to think merely of the mystery of the question, and to puzzle yourselves with arguments as to how the Three Persons are one; for that is not to think of the Ever-blessed Trinity, but only to think about it. Still less are you to think of the Ever-blessed Trinity under names of philosophy which God has not given to himself; for that is not to think of the Ever-blessed Trinity at all. You must think of the Ever-blessed Trinity as he is,—of a Father, a Son, and a Holy Spirit; and to think of him the more earnestly, the more you are sad at heart. It may be that God has sent that sadness to make you think of him. It may be that God has cut the very ground from under your feet that you may rest on him, the true and only ground of all created things; as it is written: 'Who is 'he among you who walketh in darkness 'and hath no light? Let him trust in the 'name of the Lord, and stay upon his 'God.'

Some will tell you, that if you are sorrowful it is a time for self-examination, and for thinking of your own soul. I answer—In good time, but not yet. Think first of God; for how can you ever know anything rightly about your own soul unless you first know rightly concerning God, in whom your soul lives, and moves, and has its being?

Others may tell you to think of God's dealings with his people. I answer—In good time, but not yet; think first of God. For how can you rightly understand God's dealings, unless you first rightly understand who God is, and what his character is? Right notions concerning your own soul, right notions concerning God's dealings, can only come from right notions concerning God himself. He is before all things. Think of him before all things. He is the first, and he is the last. Think of him first in this life, and so you will think of him last, and for ever in the life to come. Think of the Father, that he is a Father indeed, in spirit and in truth. Think of the Son, that he is a Son indeed, in spirit and in truth. Think of the Holy Spirit, that he is a Holy Spirit indeed, in spirit and in truth. So you will be thinking indeed of the Everblessed Trinity; and will worship God, not with your lips or your thoughts merely, but in spirit and in truth. Think of the Father, that he is the Father of our Lord Jesus Christ, and that the perfect Son must be for ever perfectly like the perfect Father. For then you will believe that God the Father looks on you, and feels for you, exactly as does Jesus Christ your Lord; then you will feel that he is a Father indeed; and will enter more and more into the unspeakable comfort of that word of all words, 'Our Father who art in heaven.'

Think of the Lord Jesus Christ as the perfect Son, who, though he is co-equal and co-eternal with his Father, yet came not to do his own will, but his Father's; who instead of struggling, instead of helping himself, cried in his agony: 'Not my will, but thine be done;' and conquered by resignation. So you will enter into the unspeakable comfort of conquering by resignation, as you see that your resignation is to be like the resignation of Christ; not that of trembling fear like a condemned criminal before a judge; not that of sullen necessity, like a slave before his master: but that of the only-begotten Son of God; the resignation of a child to the will of a father whom he can utterly trust, because that father's name is love.

Think of the Holy Spirit as a person; having a will of his own; who breatheth whither he listeth, and cannot be confined to any feelings or rules of yours, or of any man's; but may meet you in the Sacraments, or out of the Sacraments, even as he will; and has methods of comforting and educating you, of which you will never dream; one whose will is the same as the will of the Father and of the Son, even a good will; just as his character is the same as the character of the Father and of the Son: even love which works by holiness; love which you can trust utterly, for yourself and for all whom you love.

Think, I say, of God himself as he is; think of his name, by which he has revealed himself, and thus you will——But who am I, to pretend to tell you what you will learn by thinking rightly of Father, Son, and Holy Ghost? How can I dare to say how much you will or will not learn? How can I put bounds to God's teaching? to the workings of him who has said, 'If a man love me, he 'will keep my words, and my Father will 'love him; and we will come unto him, and 'make our abode with him'? How can I tell you in a few words of one sermon all that that means? How can I, or any man, know all that that means? Who is one man, or all men, to exhaust the riches of the glory of God, or the blessings which may come from thinking of God's glory? Let it be enough for us to be sure that truly to know God is everlasting life; and that the more we think of God by his own revealed name of Father, Son, and Holy Ghost, the more we shall enter, now and hereafter, into eternal life, and into the peace which comes by the true knowledge of him in whom we live, and move, and have our being.

SERMON VIII.

THE END OF RELIGION.

Ephesians iv. 23, 24.

Be renewed in the spirit of your mind; and put ye on the new man, which after God is created in righteousness and true holiness.

THIS text is exceedingly valuable to us; for it tells us the end and aim of all religion. It tells us why we are to pray, whether at home or in church; why we are to read our Bibles and good books; why we are to be what is commonly called religious.

It tells us, I say, the end and aim of all religion; namely, that we may put on 'the new man, which after God'—according to the likeness of God—'is created in righteousness and true holiness.' So says St. Paul in another place: 'Be ye therefore followers'—

literally, copiers, imitators—'of God, as dear children.'

Now this is not what you will be told from too many pulpits, and in too many books, now-a-days, is the end of religion. You will be told that the end of religion is to save your soul, and go to heaven.

But experience shows, my friends, in all religions and in all ages, that those who make it their first object in life to save their souls, are but too likely to lose them; as our Lord says, He that saveth his soul, or life—for the words are the same in Scripture—shall lose it.

And experience shows that in all religions, and in all ages, those who make it their first object in life to get to heaven, are but too likely never to get there: because in their haste, they forget what heaven is, and what is the only way of arriving at it.

Good works, as they call the likeness of God and the Divine life, are in too many persons' eyes only fruits of faith, or proofs of faith, and not the very end of faith, and of religion—ay, of their very existence here on earth; and therefore they naturally begin to ask,—How few good works will be enough to prove their faith? And when a man has once set that question before himself, he is sure to find a comfortable answer, and to discover that very few good works indeed,—a very little sanctification (as it is called), a very little righteousness, and a very little holiness,—will be enough to save his soul, as far at least as he wishes his soul to be saved. My friends, all this springs from that selfish view of religion which is gaining power among us more and more. Christ came to deliver us from our selfishness; from being slaves to our selfish prudence and selfish interest. But we make religion a question of profit and loss, as we make everything else. We ask—What shall I get by being good? What shall I get by worshipping God? Is it not prudent, and self-interested, and business-like to give up a little pleasure on earth, in the hope of getting a great deal in heaven? Is not religion a good investment? Is it not, considering how short and uncertain life is, the best of all life-insurances?

THE END OF RELIGION.

My friends, we who have to earn our bread and to take honest money for honest work, know well enough what trouble we have to keep out of our daily life that mean, base spirit of self-interest, rather than of duty, which never asks of anything, 'Is it right?' but only 'Will it pay me?'—which, instead of thinking, How can I do this work as well as possible? is perpetually thinking, How can I get most money for the least work? We have to fight against that spirit in worldly matters. For we know, that if we yield to it,—if we sacrifice our duty to our pleasure or our gain,—it is certain to make us do something mean, covetous, even fraudulent, in the eyes of God and man.

But if we carry that spirit into religion, and our spiritual and heavenly duties; if we forget that that is the spirit of the world; if we forget that we renounced the world at our baptism, and that we therefore promised not to shape our lives by *its* rules and maxims; if our thought is, not of whatsoever things are just, whatsoever things are pure, whatsoever things are lovely, of good report, whatsoever brings us true honour and deserved praise from God and from man; if we think only that intensely selfish and worldly thought, How much will God take for saving my soul?—which is the secret thought (alas that it should be so!) of too many of all denominations,—then we shall be in a fair way of killing our souls; so that if they be saved, they will not at all events be saved alive. For we shall kill in our souls just those instincts of purity, justice, generosity, mercy, love, in one word, of unselfishness and unworldliness, which make the very life of the soul, because they are inspired by the Spirit of God, even the Holy Ghost. And we shall be but too likely not to sit in heavenly places with Christ Jesus—as St. Paul tells us we may do even in this life: but to go to our own place—wherever that may be—with selfish Judas, who when he found that his Saviour was not about to restore the kingdom to Israel, and make a great prince of him there and then, made the best investment he could, under the danger which he saw at hand, by selling his Lord for thirty pieces of silver: to remain to all time a warning to those who are religious for self-interest's sake.

What, then, is the end and aim of true Religion? St. Paul tells us in the text. The end and aim, he says, of hearing Christ, the end and aim of learning the truth as it is in Jesus, is this—that we may be renewed in the spirit of our minds, and put on the new man, which after God is created in righteousness and true holiness. To put on the new man; the new pattern of manhood, which is after the pattern of the Son of man, Jesus Christ, and therefore after the pattern and likeness of God. To be followers, that is, copiers and imitators of God, that (so says St. Paul) is the end and aim of religion. In one word, we are to be good; and religion, according to St. Paul, is neither more nor less than the act of becoming good, like the good God.

To be like God. Can we have any higher and more noble aim than that? And yet it is a simple aim. There is nothing fantastic, fanatical, inhuman about it. It is within our reach—within the reach of every man and woman; within the reach of the poorest, the most unlearned. For how does St. Paul tell us that we can become like God?

'Wherefore,' he says, 'putting away lying,
'speak every man truth with his neighbour:
'for we are members one of another. Be
'ye angry, and sin not: let not the sun go
'down upon your wrath: neither give place
'to the devil. Let him that stole steal no
'more: but rather let him labour, working
'with his hands the thing which is good,
'that he may have to give to him that
'needeth. Let no corrupt communication
'proceed out of your mouth, but that which
'is good to the use of edifying, that it may
'minister grace unto the hearers. And grieve
'not the Holy Spirit of God, whereby ye are
'sealed unto the day of redemption. Let
'all bitterness, and wrath, and anger, and
'clamour, and evil speaking, be put away
'from you, with all malice: and be ye kind
'one to another, tender-hearted, forgiving one
'another, even as God for Christ's sake hath
'forgiven you.'

Do that, he says, and you will be followers of God, as dear children; and thus will you surely save your souls alive. For they will be inspired by the Spirit of God, the spirit of goodness, who is the Lord and Giver of life; wherefore they cannot decay nor die, but must live and grow, develop and improve perpetually, becoming better and wiser,—and therefore more useful to their fellow-creatures, more blessed in themselves, and more pleasing to God their Father, through all eternity. And thus you will surely go to heaven. For heaven will begin on earth, and last on after this earth, and all that binds you to this earth, has vanished in the grave.

Heaven will begin on earth, I say. When St. Paul told these very Ephesians to whom my text was addressed, that God had made them sit, even then, in heavenly places with Christ Jesus, he did not mean in any wise— what they would have known was not true— that their bodies had been miraculously lifted up above the earth, above the clouds, or elsewhere: no, for he had told them before, in the first chapter, what he meant by heavenly places. God their Father, he says, had blessed them with all spiritual blessings in heavenly places, in Christ, in that He had chosen them in Christ before the foundation of the world—and for what end? For the very end which I have been preaching to you. 'That they should be holy, and without blame before God, in Love.' That was heaven. If they were that,—holy, blameless, loving, they were in heavenly places already,—in that moral and spiritual heaven in which God abides for ever. They were with God, and with all who are like God, as it is written, 'He that dwelleth in love, dwelleth in God, and God in him.'

My dear friends, this is the heaven for which we are all to strive—a heaven of goodness, wherein God dwells. And therefore an eternal and everlasting heaven, as eternal as goodness and as eternal as God himself; and if we are living in it, we have all we need. But we may begin to live in it here. To what particular place our souls go after death, Scripture does not tell us, and we need not know. To what particular place our souls and bodies go after the resurrection, Scripture tells us not, and we need not know. But this Scripture tells us, and that is enough for us, that they will be in heavenly places, in the presence of Christ and of God. And this Scripture tells us—and indeed our own conscience and reason tell us likewise—that though death may alter our place, it cannot alter our character; though it may alter the circumstances round us, it cannot alter ourselves. If we have been good and pure before death, we shall be good and pure after death. If we have been led and inspired by God's Spirit before death, so shall we be after death. If we have been in heavenly places before death, thinking heavenly thoughts, feeling heavenly feelings, and doing heavenly deeds, then we shall be in heavenly places after death; for we shall have with us the Spirit of God, whose presence is heaven; and as long as we are holy, good, pure, unselfish, just, and merciful, we may be persuaded, with St. Paul, that wheresoever we go, all will be well; for 'neither 'death, nor life, nor angels, nor powers, nor

'things present, nor things to come, nor
'height, nor depth, nor any other creature,
'shall be able to separate us from the love
'of God, which is in Christ Jesus our
'Lord.'

SERMON IX.

THE HUMANITY OF GOD.

St. Luke xv. 7.

I say unto you, that likewise joy shall be in heaven over one sinner that repenteth, more than over ninety and nine just persons, which need no repentance.

THERE are three parables in this chapter: all agree in one quality—in their humanity. God shows us in them that there is something in his character which is like the best and simplest parts of our characters. God himself likens himself to men, that men may understand him and love him.

Why there should be more joy over the repenting sinner than over the just man who needs no repentance, we cannot explain in words: but our hearts tell us that it is true, beautiful; that it is reasonable, though we can give no reason for it. You know that if you had lost a sheep; if you had lost a piece of money; if you had had a child run away from you, it would be far more pleasant to find that thing which you had lost, than never to have lost it at all. You do not know why. God tells you that it is a part of his image and likeness in you; that you rejoice over what you have lost and found again, because God rejoices over what he has lost and found again.

And is not this a gospel, and good news? Is it not good news that we need never be afraid or ashamed to give way to our tenderness and pity? for God does not think it beneath him to be tender and pitiful. Is it not good news that we need never be afraid or ashamed to forgive, to take back those who have neglected us, wronged us? for God does not think it beneath him to do likewise. That we need never show hardness, pride, sternness to our children when they do wrong, but should win them by love and tenderness, caring for them all the more, the less they care for themselves? for God does even so to us, who have sinned against him far more than our children ever can sin against us.

And is it not good news, again, that God does care for sinners, and for all kinds and sorts of sinners? Some go wrong from mere stupidity and ignorance, because they know no better; because they really are not altogether accountable for their own doings. They are like the silly sheep, who gets out over the fence of his own fancy: and yet no reasonable man will be angry with the poor thing. It knows no better. How many a poor young thing goes wandering away, like that silly sheep, and having once lost its way, cannot get back again, but wanders on further and further, till it lies down all desperate, tired out, mired in the bogs, and torn about with thorns!

Then the good shepherd does not wait for that sheep to come back. He goes and seeks it far and wide, up hill and down dale, till he finds it; and having found it, he does not beat it, rate it—not even drive it home before him. It is tired and miserable. If it has been foolish, it has punished itself enough for its folly; and all he feels for it is pity and love. It wants rest, and he gives it rest at his own expense. He lays it on his shoulders, and takes it home, calling on all heaven and earth to rejoice with him. Ah, my friends, if that is not the picture of a God whom you can love, of a God whom you can trust, what God would you have?

Some, again, go wrong from ignorance and bad training, bad society, bad education, bad example; and in other countries—though, thank God, not in this—from bad laws and bad government. How many thousands and hundreds of thousands are ruined, as it seems to us, thereby! The child born in a London alley, reared up among London thieves, taught to swear, lie, steal, never entering a school or church, never hearing the name of God save in oaths—There is the lost piece of money. It is a valuable thing; the King's likeness is stamped on it: but it is useless, because it is lost, lying in the dust and darkness, hidden in a corner, unable to help itself, and of no use to any one. And so there is many a person, man and woman, who is worth something, who has God's likeness on them, who, if they were brought home to God, might be of good use in the world; but they are lost, from ignorance and bad training. They lie in a corner in darkness, not knowing their own value in God's eyes; not knowing that they bear his image, though it be all crusted over with the dust and dirt of barbarism and bad habits. Then Christ will go after them, and seek diligently till he finds them, and cleanses them, and makes them bright, and of good use again in his Church and his kingdom. They are worth something, and Christ will not let them be wasted; he will send clergymen, teachers, missionaries, schools, reformatories, penitentiaries, hospitals—ay, and other messengers of his, of whom we never dream, for his ways are as high above our ways as the heaven is above the earth: with all these he sweeps his house, and his blessing is on them all, for by them he finds the valuable coin which was lost.

But there is a third sort of sinner, spoken of in Christ's next parable in this chapter, from which my text is taken, of whom it is not said that God the Father sends out to seek and to save him. That is the prodigal son, who left his father's house, and strayed away of his own wantonness and free will. Christ does not go out after him. He has gone away of his own will; and of his own will he must come back: and he has to pay a heavy price for his folly—to taste hunger, shame, misery, all but despair. For understand—if any of you fancy that you can sin without being punished—that the prodigal son is punished, and most severely. He does not get off freely, the moment he chooses to repent, as false preachers will tell you: even after he does repent, and resolves to go back to his father's house, he has a long journey home, in poverty and misery, footsore, hungry, and all but despairing. But when he does get home; when he shows that he has learnt the bitter lesson; when all he dares to ask is, 'Make me as one of thy hired servants,' he is received as freely as the rest. And it is worth while to remark, that our Lord spends on him tenderer words than on those who are lost by mere foolishness or ignorance. Of him it is not said, 'Rejoice with me, for I have found him,' —but, Bring out the best robe, for this my son—not my sheep, not my piece of money, but my son—was dead, and is alive again; he was lost, and is found.

In this is a great mystery; one of which one hardly dares to talk: but one which one must think over in one's own heart, and say, 'Oh the depth of the riches and of the know-'ledge and wisdom of God! How wonderful 'are his judgments, and his ways past finding 'out. For who hath known the mind of the 'Lord, or who hath been his counsellor? Or 'who hath first given to him, and it shall be 'recompensed unto him again?' Who indeed? God is not a tyrant, who must be appeased with gifts; or a taskmaster, who must be satisfied with the labour of his slaves. He is a father who loves his children; who gives, and loveth to give; who gives to all freely, and upbraideth not. He truly willeth not the death of a sinner, but rather that he should turn from his wickedness and live. His will is a good will; and howsoever much man's sin and folly may resist it, and seem for a time to mar it, yet he is too great and good to owe any man, even the worst, the smallest spite or grudge. Patiently, nobly, magnanimously, God waits; waits for the man who is a fool, to find out his own folly; waits for the heart which has tried to find pleasure in everything else, to find out that everything else disappoints, and to come back to him, the fountain of all wholesome pleasure, the well-spring of all life fit for a man to live. When the fool finds out his folly; when the wilful man gives up his wilfulness; when the rebel submits himself to law; when the son comes back to his father's house —there is no sternness, no peevishness, no upbraiding, no pride, no revenge; but the everlasting and boundless love of God wells forth again as rich as ever. He has condescended to wait for his creature; because what he wanted was not his creature's fear, but his creature's love; not his lip-obedience, but his heart; because he wanted him not to come back as a trembling slave to his master, but as a son who has found out at last what a father he has left him, when all beside has played him false. Let him come back thus; and then all is forgiven and forgotten; and all that will be said will be, 'This my son was dead, 'and is alive again; he was lost, and is 'found.'

SERMON X.

GOD'S WORLD.

(Preached before the Prince of Wales, at Sandringham, 1866.)

GENESIS I. I.

In the beginning God created the heaven and the earth.

IT may seem hardly worth while to preach upon this text. Every one thinks that he believes it. Of course—they say—we know that God made the world. Teach us something we do not know, not something which we do. Why preach to us about a text which we fully understand, and believe already?

Because, my friends, there are few texts in the Bible more difficult to believe than this, the very first; few texts which we need to repeat to ourselves again and again, in all the chances and changes of this mortal life; lest we should forget it just as we feel we are most sure of it.

We know that it was very difficult for people in olden times to believe it. Else why did all the heathens of old, and why do all heathens now, worship idols?

We know that the old Jews, after it had been revealed to them, found it very difficult to believe it. Else why were they always deserting the worship of God, and worshipping idols and devils, sun, moon, and stars, and all the host of heaven?

We know that the early Christians, in spite of the light of the Gospel and of God's Spirit, found it very difficult to believe it. Doubtless they believed it a thousand times more fully than it had ever been believed before. They would have shrunk with horror from saying that any one but God had made the heavens and the earth. But Christians clung, for many hundred years, even almost up to our own day, to old heathen superstitions, which they would have cast away if their faith had been full, and if they had held with their whole hearts and souls and minds, that there was one God, of whom are all things. They believed that the Devil and evil spirits had power to raise thunderstorms, and blight crops, and change that course of nature of which the Psalmist had said, that all things served God, and continued this day as at the beginning, for God had given them a law which could not be broken. They believed in magic, and astrology, and a hundred other dreams, which all began from secret disbelief that God made the heaven and the earth; till they fancied that the Devil could and would teach men the secrets of nature, and the way to be rich and great, if they would but sell their souls to him. They believed, in a word, the very atheistic lie which Satan told to our blessed Lord, when he said that all the kingdoms of the world and the glory of them were his, and to whomsoever he would he gave them—instead of believing our Lord's answer, 'Get thee behind me, Satan: it is 'written, Thou shalt worship the Lord thy ' God, and him only shalt thou serve.'

And therefore I tell you here—as the Church has told Christian people in all ages

—that if any of you have any fancy for such follies, any belief in charms and magic, any belief that you can have your fortunes told by astrologers, gipsies, or such like, you must go back to your Bible, and learn better the first text in it. 'In the beginning God created the heaven and the earth.' God's is the kingdom, and the power, and the glory, of all things visible and invisible; all the world round us, with its wonderful secrets, is governed, from the sun over our heads, to the smallest blade of grass beneath our feet, by God, and by God alone, and neither evil spirit nor magician has the smallest power over one atom of it; and our fortunes, in like wise, do not depend on the influences of stars or planets, ghosts or spirits, or anything else: but on ourselves, of whom it is written, that God shall judge every man according to his works.

Even now, in these very days, many good people are hardly able, it seems to me, to believe with their whole hearts that God made heaven and earth. They half believe it: but their faith is weak; and when it is tried, they grow frightened, and afraid of truth. This it is which makes so many good people afraid of what is now called Science—of all new discoveries about the making of this earth, and the powers and virtues of the things about us; afraid of wonders which are become matters of course among us, but of which our forefathers knew little or nothing. They are afraid lest these things should shake people's faith in the Bible, and in Christianity; lest men should give up the good old faith of their forefathers, and fancy that the world is grown too wise to believe in the old doctrines. One cannot blame them, cannot even be surprised at them. So many wonderful truths (for truths they are), of which our fathers never dreamed, are discovered every year, that none can foretell where the movement will stop; what we shall hear next; what we shall have to believe next.

Only, let us take refuge in the text—' In ' the beginning God created the heaven and ' the earth.' All that we see around us, however wonderful; all that has been found out of late, however wonderful; all that will be ever found out, however still more wonderful it may be, is the work of God; of that God who revealed himself to Moses; of that God who led the children of Israel out of their slavery in Egypt; of that God who taught David, in all his trouble and wanderings, to trust in him as his guide and friend; of that God who revealed to the old Prophets the fate of nations, and the laws by which he governs all the kingdoms and people of the earth; of that God, above all, who so loved the world, that he gave his only begotten Son, that the world by him might be saved.

This material world which we do see, is as much God's world as the spiritual world we do not see. And, therefore, the one cannot contradict the other; and the true understanding of the one will never hurt our true understanding of the other.

But many good people have another fear, and that, I think, a far more serious one. They are afraid, in consequence of all these wonderful discoveries of science, that people will begin to trust in science, and not in God. And that fear is but too well founded. It is certain that if sinful man can find anything to trust in, instead of God, trust therein he surely will.

The old Jews preferred to trust in idols, rather than God; the Christians of the Middle Age, to their shame, trusted in magic and astrology, rather than God; and after that, some 200 years ago, when men had grown too wise to trust in such superstitions, they certainly did not grow wise enough, most of them, to trust in the living God. They relied, the rulers of the nations especially, in their own wit and cunning, and tried to govern the world and keep it straight, by falsehood and intrigue, envy and jealousy, plotting and party spirit, and the wisdom which cometh not from above, but is earthly, sensual, devilish,—that wisdom against which we pray, whenever we sing 'God save the Queen,'—

> 'Confound their politics,
> Frustrate their knavish tricks,
> On Thee our hopes we fix,
>   GOD save the Queen.'

And since that false wisdom has failed, and the wisdom of this world, and the rulers of this world, came to nought in the terrible crisis of the French Revolution, eighty years ago, men have been taking up a new idolatry. For as science has spread, they have been trusting in science rather than in the living God, and giving up the old faith that God's judgments are in all the earth, and that he rewards righteousness and punishes iniquity; till too many seem to believe that the world somehow made itself, and that there is no living God ordering and guiding it; but that a man must help himself as he best can in this world, for in God no help is to be found.

And how shall we escape that danger?

I do not think we shall escape it, if we stop short at the text. We must go on from the Old Testament and let the New explain it. We must believe what Moses tells us: but we must ask St. John to show us more than Moses saw. Moses tells us that God created the heavens and the earth; St. John goes further, and tells us what that God is like; how he saw Christ, the Word of God, by whom all things were made, and without whom nothing was made that is made. And what was he like? He was the brightness of his Father's glory, and the express image of his person. And what was that like? was there any darkness in him—meanness, grudging, cruelty, changeableness, deceit? No. He was full of grace and truth. Grace and truth: that is what Christ is; and therefore that is what God is.

There was another aspect of him, true; and St. John saw that likewise. And so awful was it that he fell at the Lord's feet as he had been dead.

But the Lord was still full of grace and truth; still, however awful he was, he was as full as ever of love, pity, gentleness. He was the Lamb that was slain for the sins of the world, even though that Lamb was in the midst of the throne from which came forth thunderings and lightnings, and judgments against the sins of all the world. Terrible to wrong, and to the doers of wrong: but most loving and merciful to all true penitents, who cast themselves and the burden of their sins before his feet; perfect justice and perfect Love,—that is God. That is the maker of this world. That is he who in the beginning made heaven and earth. An utterly good God. A God whose mercy is over all his creatures. A God who desires the good of his creatures; who willeth not that one little one should perish; who will have all men to be saved, and to come to the knowledge of the truth; who wages everlasting war against sin and folly, and wrong and misery, and all the ills to which men are heirs; who not only made the world, but loves the world, and who proved that—what a proof!—by not sparing his only-begotten Son, but freely giving him for us.

Therefore we can say, not merely,—I know that a God made the world, but I know what that God is like. I know that he is not merely a great God, a wise God, but a good God; that goodness is his very essence. I know that he is gracious and merciful, long suffering, and of great kindness. I know that he is loving to every man, and that his mercy is over all his works. I know that he upholds those who fall, and lifts up those who are down; I know that he careth for the fatherless and widow, and executes judgment and justice for all those who are oppressed with wrong. I know that he will fulfil the desire of those who call upon him; and will also hear their cry and will help them. I know, in short, that he is a living God, and a loving God; a God in whom men may trust, to whom they may open their hearts, as children to their father: and I am sure that those who come to him he will in no wise cast out; for he himself has said, with human voice upon this earth of ours,—'Come unto me, all 'ye that labour and are heavy laden and I 'will give you rest.'

In him all can trust. The sick man on his bed can trust in him and say—In the beginning God created the heaven and the earth; and he is full of grace and truth. This sickness of mine comes by the laws of heaven and earth; and those laws are God's laws. Then even this sickness may be full of grace and truth. It comes by no blind chance, but by the will of him who so loved me, that he stooped to die for me on the Cross. Christ my Lord and God has some gracious and bountiful purpose in it, some lesson for me to learn from it. I will ask him to teach me that lesson; and I trust in him that he will teach me; and that, even for this sickness and this sorrow, I shall have cause to thank him in the world to come. Shall I not trust him who not only made this world, but so loved it that he stooped to die for it upon the Cross?

The labourer and the farmer can trust in him, in the midst of short crops and bad seasons, and say, In the beginning God created the heaven and the earth; and he is full of grace and truth. Frost and blight obey his commands as well as sunshine and plenty. He knows best what ought to be. Shall we not trust in him, who not only made this world, but so loved it, that he stooped to die for it upon the Cross?

The scholar and the man of science, studying the wonders of this earth, can trust in him, and say, In the beginning God created the heaven and the earth; and he is full of grace and truth. Many things puzzle me; and the more I learn the less I find I **really** know: but I shall know as much as is good for me, and for mankind. God is full of grace, and will not grudge me knowledge; and full of truth, and will not deceive me. And I shall never go far wrong as long as I believe, not only in one God, the Father Almighty, Maker of all things visible and invisible, but in one Lord Jesus Christ, his only-begotten Son, light of light, very God of very God, by whom all things were made, who for us men and our salvation came down, and died, and rose again; whose kingdom shall have no end; who rules over every star and planet, every shower and sunbeam, every plant and animal and stone, every body and every soul of man; who will teach men, in his good time and way, all that they need know, in order to multiply and replenish the earth, and subdue it in this life, and attain everlasting life in the world to come. And for the rest, puzzled though I be, shall I not trust him, who not only made this world, but so loved it, that he stooped to die for it upon the Cross?

SERMON XI.

THE ARMOUR OF GOD.

(Preached before the Prince of Wales, at Sandringham, January 20th, 1867.)

EPHESIANS VI. 11.

Put on the whole armour of God.

ST. PAUL again and again compares himself and the Christians to whom he writes to soldiers, and their lives to warfare. And it was natural that he should do so. Everywhere he went, in those days, he would find Roman soldiers, ruling over men of different races from themselves, and ruling them, on the whole, well. Greeks, Syrians, Jews, Egyptians,—all alike in his days obeyed the Roman soldiers, who had conquered the then known world.

And St. Paul and his disciples wished to

conquer the world likewise. The Roman soldier had conquered it for Cæsar: St. Paul would conquer it for Christ. The Roman soldier had used bodily force—the persuasion of the sword. St. Paul would use spiritual force—the persuasion of preaching. The Roman soldier wrestled against flesh and blood: St. Paul wrestled against more subtle and dangerous enemies—spiritual enemies, he calls them—who enslaved and destroyed the reason, and conscience, and morals of men.

St. Paul and his disciples, I say, had set before themselves no less a task than to conquer the world.

Therefore, he says, they must copy the Roman soldier, and put on their armour, as he put on his. He took Cæsar's armour, and put on Cæsar's uniform. They must take the armour of God, that they may withstand in the evil day of danger and battle, and having done all,—done their duty manfully as good soldiers,—stand; keep their ranks, and find themselves at the end of the battle not scattered and disorganized, but in firm and compact order, like the Roman soldiers, who, by drill and discipline, had conquered the irregular and confused troops of all other nations.

Let me, this morning, explain St. Paul's words to you, one by one. We shall find them full of lessons—and right wholesome lessons—for in this parable of the armour of God St. Paul sketches what you and I and every man should be. He sketches the character of a good man, a true man, a man after God's own heart.

First, the Christians are to gird their loins—to cover the lower part of their body, which is the most defenceless. That the Roman soldier did with a kilt, much like that which the Highlanders wear now. And that garment was to be Truth. Truthfulness, honesty, that was to be the first defence of a Christian man, instead of being, as too many so-called Christians make it, the very last. Honesty, before all other virtues, was to gird his very loins, was to protect his very vitals.

The breastplate, which covered the upper part of the body, was to be righteousness—

which we now commonly call, justice. To be a just man, after being first a truthful man, was the Christian's duty.

And his helmet was to be the hope of Salvation—that is, of safety: not merely of being saved in the next world—though of course St. Paul includes that—but of being saved in this world; of coming safe through the battle of life; of succeeding; of conquering the heathen round them, and making them Christians, instead of being conquered by them. The hope of safety was to be his helmet, to guard his head—the thinking part. We all know how a blow on the head confuses and paralyses a man, making him (as we say) lose his head. We know too, how, in spiritual matters, terror and despair deal a deadly blow to a man's mind,—how if a man expects to fail, he cannot think clearly and calmly,—how often desperation and folly go hand in hand; for, if a man loses hope, he is but too apt to lose his reason. The Christian's helmet, then,—that which would save his head, and keep his mind calm, prudent, strong, and active,—was the hope of success.

And for their feet—they must be shod with the preparation of the Gospel of peace.

That is a grand saying, if you will remember that the key-word, which explains it all, is Peace, and the Gospel, that is, the good news, thereof.

The Roman soldier had his preparation, which kept him prepared and ready to march through the world; and of that St. Paul was thinking, and had need to think; for he had heard the sound of it in every street, on every high road, from Jerusalem to Ephesus, ever since he was a child—the tramp of the heavy nailed boot which the Roman soldier always wore. The Roman soldiers were proud of their boots,—so proud that, in St. Paul's time, they nicknamed one of their royal princes Caligula, because, as a boy in camp, he used to wear boots like the common soldiers: and he bore that name when he became emperor, and bears it to this day. And they had reason to be proud, after their own notion of glory. For that boot had carried them through desert and through cities, over mountain ranges, through trackless forests, from

Africa even into Britain here, to be the conquerors of the then known world; and, wherever the tramp of that boot had been heard, it had been the sound, not of the good news of peace, but of the evil news of war. Isaiah of old, watching for the deliverance of the Jews from captivity, heard in the spirit the footsteps of the messengers coming with the news that Cyrus was about to send the Jews home to their own land, and cried, 'How beautiful upon the mountains are the 'feet of them that bring good tidings, that 'publish peace!' But the tramp of the Roman armies had as yet brought little but bad tidings, and published destruction. Men slain in battle, women and children driven off captive, villages burnt, towns. sacked and ruined, till wherever their armies passed—as one of their own writers has said—they made a desert, and then called that peace.

So had the Roman soldier marched over the world, and conquered it. And now Christ's soldiers were beginning their march over the world, that they might conquer it by fulfilling Isaiah's prophecy. They were going forth, with their feet shod with the good news of Peace ; to treat all men, not as their enemies, not as their slaves, but as their brothers ; and to bring them good news, and bid them share in it,—the good news that God was at peace with them, and that they might now be at peace with their own consciences, and at peace with each other, for all were brothers in Jesus Christ their Lord.

Shod with that good news of peace, these Christians were going to conquer the world, and to penetrate into distant lands from which the Roman armies had been driven back in shameful defeat. To penetrate, too, where the Roman armies never cared to go,—among the miserable and crowded lanes of the great cities, and conquer there what the Roman armies could not conquer—the vice, the misery, the cruelty, the idolatry of the heathen.

The shield, again, guarded those parts of the soldier which the armour did not guard. It warded off the stones, arrows, and darts— fiery darts often, as St. Paul says, which were hurled at him from afar. And the Christian's shield, St. Paul says, was to be Faith,—trust in God,—belief that he was fighting God's battle, and not his own; belief that God was over him in the battle, and would help and guide him, and give him strength to do his work. To believe firmly that he was in the right, and on God's side. To believe that, when he was wounded and struck down,— when men deserted him, cursed him, tried to take his life—perhaps did take his life—with torments unspeakable,—to have faith to say in his heart, 'I am in the right.' When he was writhing under the truly fiery darts of misrepresentation, slander, scorn, or under the equally fiery darts of remorse for his own mistakes, his own weaknesses, still to say after all, 'I am in the right.' That shield of faith, though it might not save him from wounds, torturing wounds, perhaps crippling wounds, would at least save his life,—at least protect his vitals; and, when he seemed stricken to the very earth, he could still shelter himself under that shield of faith, and cry, 'Rejoice not against 'me, O mine enemy; when I fall, I shall 'arise.'

And they were to take a sword. They were

to use only one weapon, as the Roman soldier used but one. For, though he went into battle armed with a short heavy pike, he hurled it at once against the enemy; then he closed in with his sword, and fought the real battle with that alone, hand to hand, and knee to knee. The short Roman sword, used by brave men in close fight, had defeated all the weapons of all the nations. St. Paul knew that fact, as well as we; and I cannot but suppose that he had it in his mind when he wrote these great words, and that he meant to bid Christians, when they fought God's battle, to fight, like the Romans, hand to hand: not to indulge in cowardly stratagems, intrigues, and lawyers' quibbles, fighting like the barbarians, cowardly and afar off, hurling stones, and shooting clouds of arrows, but to grapple with their enemies, looking them boldly in the face, as honest men should do, trying their strength against them fairly, and striking them to the heart. But with what? With that sword which, if it wound, heals likewise,—if it kills, also makes alive; the sword which slays the sins of a man, that he may die to sin, but rise again to righteousness; the sword of the Spirit, which is the Word of God, the message of God, the speech of God, the commandment of God. They were to conquer the world simply by saying, 'Thus saith the Lord.' They were to preach God, and God alone, revealed in his Son, Jesus Christ, a God of love, who willed that none should perish, but that all should come to the knowledge of the truth.

But a God of wrath likewise. We must never forget that. A merely indulgent God would be an unjust God, and a cruel God likewise. If God be just, as he is, then he has boundless pity for those who are weak: but boundless wrath for the strong who misuse the weak. Boundless pity for those who are ignorant, misled, and out of the right way: but boundless wrath for those who mislead them, and put them out of the right way. All through St. Paul's Epistles, as through our blessed Lord's sayings and doings, you see this wholesome mixture of severity and mercy, of Divine anger and Divine love, very different from the sentimentalism of our own times, when men fancy that, because they dislike the pain and trouble of punishing evildoers, God is even such a one as themselves, who sits still and takes no heed of the wrong which is done on earth.

No. The Christians were to tell men of both sides of God's character; for both were working every day, and all day long, about them. They were to tell men that God had, by their mouths, revealed from heaven his wrath against all ungodliness and unrighteousness of men, at the same moment that he had revealed the good news that men might be purified by the blood of Christ, and saved from wrath through him. They were to tell men of a God who so loved the world that he gave his only-begotten Son to die for it; but of a God who so loved the world that he would not tolerate in it those sins which cause the ruin of the world. Tribulation and anguish upon every soul of man that doeth evil, and glory, honour, and peace to every man that worketh good—that was to be their message, that was to be their weapon, wherewith they were to strike, and did strike, through the hearts of sinners, and convert them to repentance that they might die to sin, and live again to righteousness.

With this armour, and that one weapon, the Word of God, the Christians conquered the souls of the men of the old world. Often they failed, often they were defeated, sadly and shamefully; for they were men of like passions with ourselves. But their defeats always happened when they tried other armour than the armour of God, and fancied that they could fight the world, the flesh, and the devil with the weapons which the world, the flesh, and the devil had forged.

Still they conquered at last—for God was with them, and the Spirit of God; and they put on again and again the armour of God, *after* they had cast it off for a while to their own hurt.

And so shall we conquer in the battle of life just in proportion as we fight our battle with the armour of God.

My friends, each and all of you surely wish to succeed in life; and to succeed, not merely in getting money, still less merely in getting pleasure, but with a far nobler and far more real success. You wish, I trust, to be worthy, virtuous, respectable, useful Christian men and women; to be honoured while you live, and regretted when you die; to leave this world with the feeling that your life has not been a failure, and your years given you in vain : but that, having done some honest work at least in this world, you are going to a world where all injustice shall be set right.

Then here, in St. Paul's words, are the elements of success in life. This, and this only, is the way to true success, to put on the whole armour of God. Truthfulness, justice, peaceableness, faith in God's justice and mercy, hope of success, and the sword of the Spirit, even that word of God which, if you do not preach it to others, you can and should preach to yourselves all day long, continually asking yourselves, 'What would God have me to do? 'What is likely to be his will and message 'upon the matter which I have in hand?'— all these qualities go to make up the character of the worthy man or woman, the useful person, the truly able person, who does what he can do, well, because he is what he ought to be, good; and all these qualities you need if you will fight the battle of life like men, and conquer instead of being conquered therein.

But some will say, and with truth, 'It is easy 'to tell us to be good: we can no more change 'our own character than we can change our 'own bodies; the question is, who will make 'us good?' Who indeed, save he who said, 'Ask and ye shall receive?' St. Paul knew well enough that if his armour was God's armour, God alone could forge it, and God alone could bestow it; and therefore he ends his commands with this last command—'Pray- 'ing always, with all prayer and supplication 'in the spirit, and watching thereto with all 'perseverance, and supplication for all saints.' Those who wrote the Church Catechism knew it likewise, and have said to us from our very childhood: 'My good child, know this: that 'thou canst not do these things of thyself, nor 'walk in the commandments of God and serve 'him without his special grace; which thou 'must learn at all times to call for by diligent 'prayer.'

Yes, my friends, there is but one way to

obtain that armour of God, which will bring us safe through the battle of life; and that is, pray for it. Ask, and it shall be given to you; seek, and ye shall find; knock, and it shall be opened unto you. You who wish for true success in life, pray. Pray, if you never prayed before, morning and evening, with your whole hearts, for that Spirit of God which is truth, justice, peace, faith, and hope —and you shall not pray in vain.

SERMON XII.

PAUL AND FELIX.

Acts xxiv. 25.

And as he reasoned of righteousness, temperance, and judgment to come, Felix trembled, and answered, Go thy way for this time; when I have a convenient season, I will call for thee.

THIS is a well-known text, on which many a sermon has been preached, and with good reason, for it is an important text. It tells us of a man who, like too many men in all times, trembled when he heard the truth about his wicked life, but did not therefore repent and mend; and a very serious lesson we may draw from his example.

But even a more important fact about the text is, that it tells us what were really the fundamental doctrines of the Christian religion in those early times, about twenty-five years, seemingly, after our Lord's death; what St. Paul used to preach about; what he considered was the first thing which he had to tell men.

Let us take this latter question first. About what did St. Paul reason before Felix?

About righteousness (which means justice), temperance, and judgment to come.

I beg you to remember these words. If you believe the Bible to be inspired, you are bound to take its words as they stand. And therefore I beg you to remember that St. Paul preached not about *un*righteousness, but righteousness; not about *in*temperance, but about temperance; not about hell, but about judgment to come; in a word, not about wrong, but about right. I hope that does not seem to you a small matter. I hope that none of you are ready to say, 'It comes to the same thing in the end.' It does not come to the same thing. There is no use in telling a man what is wrong, unless you first tell him what is right. There is no use rebuking a man for being bad, unless you first tell him how he may become better, and give him hope for himself, or you will only drive him to recklessness and despair. You must show him the right road, before you can complain of him for going the wrong one.

But if St. Paul had reasoned with Felix about injustice, intemperance, and hell, one could not have been surprised. For Felix was a thoroughly bad man, unjust and intemperate, and seemingly fitting himself for hell.

He had begun life as a slave of the emperor in a court which was a mere sink of profligacy and villainy. Then he had got his freedom, and next, the governorship of Judæa, probably by his brother Pallas's interest, who had been a slave like him, and had made an enormous fortune by the most detestable wickedness.

When in his governorship, Felix began to show himself as wicked as his brother. The violence, misrule, extortion, and cruelty which went on in Judæa was notorious. He caused the high-priest at Jerusalem to be murdered out of spite. Drusilla, his wife, he had taken away from a Syrian king, who was her lawful husband. Making money seems to have been his great object; and the great Roman historian of those times sums up his character in a few bitter words thus: 'Felix,' he says, ex-'ercised the power of a king with the heart of 'a slave, in all cruelty and lust.'

Such was the wicked upstart whom God, for the sins of the Jews, had allowed to rule them in St. Paul's time; and before him St. Paul had to plead for his life.

The first time that St. Paul came before him Felix seems to have seen at once that Paul was innocent, and a good man; and that, perhaps, was the reason why he sent for him again, and, strangely enough, heard him concerning the faith in Christ.

There was some conscience left, it seems, in the wretched man. He was not easy, amid his ill-gotten honour, ill-gotten wealth, ill-gotten pleasures; and perhaps, as many men are in such a case, he was superstitious, afraid of being punished for his sins, and looking out for false prophets, smooth preachers, new religions which would make him comfortable in his sins, and drug his conscience by promising the wicked man life, where God had not promised it. So he wanted, it seems, to know what this new faith in Christ was like; and he heard.

And what he heard we may very fairly guess, because we know from St. Paul's writings what he was in the habit of saying.

St. Paul told him of righteousness—a word of which he was very fond. He told Felix of a righteous and good God, who had manifested to man his righteousness and goodness, in the righteousness and goodness of his Son Jesus; a righteous God, who wished to make all men righteous like himself, that they might be happy for ever. Perhaps St. Paul called Felix to give up all hopes of having his own righteousness —the false righteousness of forms, and ceremonies, and superstitions—and to ask for the rightousness of Christ, which is a clean heart and a right spirit; and then he set before him no doubt, as was his custom, the beauty of righteousness, the glory of it, as St. Paul calls it; how noble, honourable, divine, godlike a thing it is to be good.

Then St. Paul told Felix of temperance. And what he said we may fairly guess from his writings. He would tell Felix that there were two elements in every man, the flesh and the spirit, and that those warred against each other: the flesh trying to drag him down, that he may become a brute in fleshly lusts and passions; the spirit trying to raise him up, that he may become a son of God in purity and virtue. But if so, what need must there be of temperance! How must a man be bound to be temperate, to keep under his body and bring it into subjection, bound to restrain the lower and more brutal feelings in him, that the higher and purer feelings may grow and thrive in him to everlasting life! Truly the temperate man, the man who can restrain himself, is the only strong man, the only safe man, the only happy man, the only man worthy of the name of man at all. This, or something like this, St. Paul would have said to Felix. He did not, as far as we know, rebuke him for his sins. He left him to rebuke himself. He told him what ought to be, what he ought to do, and left the rest to his conscience. Poor Felix, brought up a heathen slave in that profligate court of Rome, had probably never heard of righteousness and temperance, had never had what was good and noble set before him. Now St. Paul set the good before him, and showed him a higher life than any he had ever dreamed of—higher than all his viceregal power and pomp—and bade him see how noble and divine it was to be good.

But it is written St. Paul reasoned with Felix about judgment to come.

We must not too hastily suppose that this means that he told Felix that he was in danger of hell-fire. For that is an argument which St. Paul never uses anywhere in his writings or speeches, as far as we know them. He never tries, as too many do now-a-days, to frighten sinners into repentance, by telling them of the flames of hell; and therefore we have no right to fancy that he did so by Felix. He told him of judgment to come; and we can guess from his writings what he would have said. That there was a living God who judged the earth always by his Son Jesus Christ, and that he was coming then, immediately, to punish all the horrible wickedness which was then going on in those parts of the world which St. Paul knew. St. Paul always speaks of the terrible judgments of God as about to come in his own days, we know that they did come.

We know—God forbid that a preacher should tell you one-tenth of what he ought to know—that St. Paul's times were the most horribly wicked that the world had ever seen; that the few heathens who had consciences left felt that some terrible punishment must come if the world went on as it was going. And we know that the punishment did come; and that for about twenty years, towards the end of which St. Paul was beheaded, the great Roman Empire was verily a hell on earth. If Felix lived ten years more he saw the judgment of God, and the vengeance of God, in a way which could not be mistaken. But did judgment to come overtake him in his life? We do not altogether know; we know that he committed such atrocities, that the Roman Emperor Nero was forced to recall him; that the chief Jews of Cæsarea sent to Rome, and there laid such accusations against him that he was in danger of death;

that his brother Pallas, who was then in boundless power, saved him from destruction. That shortly afterwards Pallas himself was disgraced, stripped of his offices, and a few years later poisoned by Nero, and it is probable enough that when he fell Felix fell with him: but we know nothing of it certainly.

But at least he saw with his own eyes that there was such a thing as judgment to come, not merely thousands of years hence at the last day, but there and then in his own lifetime. He saw the wrath of God revealed from heaven against all unrighteousness of men. He saw the wicked murdering and destroying each other till the land was full of blood. He saw the Empress-mother Agrippina, who had been the paramour of his brother Pallas, murdered by her own son, the Emperor Nero; and so judgment came on her. He saw his own brother first ruined and then poisoned; and so judgment came on him. He saw many a man whom he knew well, and who had been mixed up with him and his brother in their intrigues, put to death himself; and so judgment came on them.

And last of all he saw (unless he had died beforehand) the fall of the Emperor Nero himself—who very probably set fire to Rome, and then laid the blame on the Christians,— the man of sin, of whom St. Paul prophesied that he would be revealed—that is, unveiled, and exposed for the monster which he was; and that the Lord would destroy him with the brightness of his coming; the man who had dressed the Christians in skins, and hunted them with dogs; who had covered them with pitch, and burnt them; who had beheaded St. Paul and crucified St. Peter; who had murdered his own wife; who had put to death every good man whom he could seize, simply for being good; who had committed every conceivable sin, fault, and cruelty that can disgrace a man, while he made the people worship him as God. He saw that great Emperor Nero hunted down by his own people, who were weary of his crimes; condemned to a horrible death, hiding in a filthy hole, and at last stabbing himself in despair;

and so judgment came on him likewise; while the very heathen felt that Nero was gone to hell, leaving his name behind him as a proverb of wickedness and cruelty for ever.

So Felix, if he were alive, saw judgment come. And yet more: he saw, if he were alive, such a time follow as the world has seldom or never seen—civil war, bloodshed, lawlessness, plunder, and every horror; a time in which men longed to die and could not find death, and, instead of repenting of their evil deeds, gnawed their tongues for pain, and blasphemed the God of heaven, as St. John had prophesied in the Revelation.

Yes, if Felix lived only ten years after he trembled at St. Paul's words, he saw enough to show him that those words were true; that there was a God in heaven, whose wrath was revealed against all unrighteousness of men; who was coming out of his place to judge the earth, and punish all the tyranny and pride and profligacy and luxury of that Roman world.

God grant that he did remember St. Paul's words. God grant that he trembled once more, and to good purpose; and so repented of his sins even at the last. God grant that he may find mercy in that Day. But we can have but little hope for him; it is but too probable that he was put to death with his brother, within five years of the time when St. Paul warned him of judgment to come,—too probable that that was his last chance of salvation, and that he threw it away for ever, as too many sinners do.

What do we learn then from this sad story? We learn one most practical and important lesson, which we are all too apt to forget.

That the foundation of the Christian religion is not forms and ceremonies, nor fancies and feelings, but righteousness, temperance, and judgment to come. Judgment, I say, to come whensoever it may seem good to Christ, who sits for ever on his throne judging right, and ministering true judgment among the people. A dreadful judgment, says the Commination Service, is always hanging over the heads of those who do wrong, and always ready to fall on them, without waiting for the last day, thousands of years hence. It was by telling men that—by telling them that Christ was righteous and pure, and desired to make them righteous and pure like himself; and that Christ was a living and present judge, watching all their actions, ready at any moment to forgive their sins, and ready at any moment to punish their sins —by that message the Apostles converted the heathen. It was by believing that message, and becoming righteous and good men, temperate and pure men, and looking up in faith and hope to Christ their ever-present Judge and Lord, that the heathen were converted, and became saints and martyrs. And that religion will stand, and bring a man through the storm safe to everlasting life, while all religions which are built on doctrines and systems, on forms and ceremonies, on fancies and feelings, on the godless notion that sinners are safe enough in this life, for God will not judge and punish them till the last day, are built on a foundation of sand; and the storm when it comes will sweep those dreams away, and leave their possessors to shame and misery.

Therefore, my friends, let no man deceive you. God is not mocked. What a man soweth, that shall he reap. The wages of sin are death, as Felix found too well; but the fruit of righteousness is everlasting life, through Jesus Christ our Lord. Therefore follow after innocency, and take heed to the thing which is right; for that, and that only, shall bring a man peace at the last.

SERMON XIII.

THE GOOD SAMARITAN.

LUKE X. 33, 34.

But a certain Samaritan, as he journeyed, came where he was: and when he saw him, he had compassion on him, and went to him, and bound up his wounds, pouring in oil and wine, and set him on his own beast, and brought him to an inn, and took care of him.

NO words, perhaps, ever spoken on earth, have had more effect than those of this parable. They are words of power and of spirit; living words, which have gone forth into the hearts and lives of men, and borne fruit in them of a hundred different kinds. Truly their sound is gone out into all lands, and their words to the ends of the world, for a proof that Christ, who spake them, said truly, when he said, 'The flesh profiteth 'nothing; it is the spirit which maketh 'alive. The words which I speak unto you, 'they are spirit and they are life.'

What was the power and the spirit of this parable? What gave it its strength in the hearts of men? This—that it told them that they were to help their fellow-men, simply because they were their fellow-men. Not because they were of the same race, the same religion, the same sect or party; but simply because they were men. In a word, it commanded men to be humane; to exercise humanity; which signifies, kindness to human beings, simply because they are human beings. One can understand our Lord preaching that: it was part and parcel of his doctrine. He called himself the Son of Man. He showed what he meant by calling himself so, by the widest and most tender humanity.

But his was quite a new doctrine, and a new practice likewise. The Jews had no notion of humanity. All but themselves were common and unclean. They might not even eat with a man who was a Gentile. All mankind, save themselves, they thought, were accursed and doomed to hell. They lived, as St. Paul told them, hateful to, and hated by, all mankind. There was no humanity in them.

The Greek, again, despised all nations but his own as barbarians. He would mix with them, eat with them, work for them; but he only looked on the rest of mankind as stupid savages, out of whom he was to make money, by the basest and meanest arts. There was no humanity in him.

The Romans, again, were a thoroughly inhuman people. Their calling, they held, was to conquer all the nations of the earth, to plunder them, to enslave them. They were the great slaveholding, man-stealing people. Mercy was a virtue which they had utterly forgotten. Their public shows and games were mere butcheries of blood and torture. To see them fight to death in their theatres, pairs after pairs, sometimes thousands in one day, was the usual and regular amusement. And in that great city of Rome, which held something more than a million human beings, there was not, as far as I am aware, one single hospital, or other charitable institution of any kind. There was, in a word, no humanity in them.

But the Gospel changed all that miraculously and suddenly, both in Jew, in Greek, and in Roman. When men became Christians at St. Paul's preaching, all the old barriers of race were broken down between them. They said no more, 'I am a Roman,' 'I a Greek,' 'I a Jew,' but 'I am a Christian man; 'and, because I am a Christian, Roman and 'Greek and Jew are alike my brothers.'

There was seen such a sight as (so far as we know) was never seen before on earth— the high-born white lady worshipping by the side of her own negro slave; the proud and selfish Roman, who never had helped a human being in his life, sending his alms to the churches of Syria, or of some other country far away; the clever and educated Greek learning from the Jew, whom he called a barbarian; and the Jew, who had hated all mankind, and been hated by them in return, preaching to all mankind the good news that they were brothers, in the name and for the sake of Jesus Christ, the Son of Man.

Instead of a kingdom of division, the Church was a kingdom of union. Charity, and generosity, and mutual help took the place of selfishness, and distrust, and oppression. While men had been heathens, their pattern had been that of the priest who saw the wounded man lying, and looked on him and passed by. Their pattern now was that of the good Samaritan, who helped and saved the wounded stranger, simply because he was a man.

In one word, the new thing which the Gospel brought into the world was—humanity. The thing which the Gospel keeps in the world still, is humanity. It brought other things, and blessed things, but this it brought. And why? Because through the Church was poured on men the spirit of God. And what is that, save humanity?—the spirit of the compassionate, all generous Son of Man?—the spirit of charity and love?

What were the woes of humanity to the heathen? If a man fell in the race of life, so much the worse for him. So much the better for them, for there was one more competitor out of the way. One of the greatest Roman poets, indeed, talks of the pleasure which men have in seeing others in trouble, just as, when the storm is tossing up the sea, it is sweet to sit on the shore, and watch the ships labouring in the waves. Not, he says, that one takes actual pleasure in seeing a man in trouble, but in the thought that one is not in the trouble oneself. A rather lame excuse, I think, for a rather inhuman sentiment.

Yes, the heathen could feel pleasure in being safe while others were afflicted. And, indeed, our own fallen nature, if we give way to it, will tempt us to the same sin. But how did men begin to look not only on the afflictions, but on the interest, on the feelings, on the consciences of their neighbours, when they began to be led by the spirit of Christ? Let St. Paul speak for himself, not in one text only, but in a hundred—' Though I be free
' from all, I have made myself a servant to all
' —a Jew to the Jews, a Greek to the Greeks,
' strong to the strong, weak to the weak; all
' things to all men, if by any means I might
' save some. Whether we be afflicted, it is for
' your consolation and salvation; or whether
' we be comforted, it is for your consolation
' and salvation. For the love of Christ con-

'straineth us. For he died for all, that those who live should henceforth not live to them-'selves, but to him.'

And what did he mean by living to Christ?
—' Living in weariness and painfulness, in 'watchings often; in hunger and thirst, in 'fastings often, in cold and nakedness; beside 'that which cometh upon me daily, the care 'of all the Church. Who is weak, and I am 'not weak? Who is offended, and I burn not?'
—Oh, who does not see in such words as these the picture of a new ideal, a new life for man; even a life of utter sympathy with his fellow-men, utter love and self-sacrifice—in one word, utter humanity; as far above that old heathen poet's selfish notion, as man is above the ape, or heaven above the earth!

This is the spirit of God, even the Holy Ghost; the spirit of Christ, which also is the spirit of humanity; because it is the spirit of Christ, who is both God and man, both human and divine. This is the spirit of love, by which God created mankind and all the worlds, that he might have something which was not himself whereon to spend his boundless love. This is the spirit of love, by which he spared not his only-begotten Son, but freely gave him for the sins of all mankind. This is the spirit of love, by which he is leading mankind through strange paths, and by ways which their fathers knew not, toward that eternal city of God which all truly human hearts are seeking, blindly often and confusedly, and sometimes by utterly mistaken paths: but seeking her still, if by any means they may enter into her, and be at peace. This is that spirit of love, by which, having sent forth all souls out of his everlasting bosom, he will draw them home again in the fulness of time, as many as have eternal life in Jesus Christ our Lord, into his bosom once more, that they may rest in peace, and God be all in all.

Take comfort from these words, my friends; for there is deep comfort to be found in them, if you will look at them aright. When you hear that the spirit of God is in you, unless you are reprobates; and that if any man have not the spirit of Christ, he is none of his —do not be afraid, as if that spirit were something quite unlike anything which you feel, or even think of: as if it was something which must show itself in strange visions or peculiar experiences, which very few persons have, and which tempt them to set themselves apart from their fellow-men, and thank God that they are not as other men are. Remember that the spirit of God is the spirit of Christ, and that the spirit of Christ is the spirit by which the good Samaritan helped the poor wounded man, simply because he was a man. Remember that the spirit of God, so far from making you unlike a man, comes to make you more perfect men; so far from parting you from your fellow-men, comes to knit you more to your fellow-men, by making you understand them, feel for them, make allowances for them, long to help them, however different in habits or in opinions they may be from you; that it is, in one word, the spirit of humanity, which comes down from heaven into your hearts to make you humane, as it descended on Christ, that he might be the most humane of all human beings—the very Son of Man, who knew, understood, loved, suffered for, and redeemed all mankind, because in him all humanity was gathered into one.

That spirit is not far from any of you. Surely he is in all your hearts already, if you be worthy of the name of men. He is in you, unless you be inhuman, and that, I trust, none of you are. From him come every humane thought and feeling you ever had. All kindliness, pity, mercy, generosity; all sense or justice and honour toward your fellow-men; all indignation when you hear of their being wronged, tortured, enslaved; all desire to help the fallen, to right the oppressed;—whence do these come? From the world? Most surely not. From the flesh? St. Paul says not. From the Devil? No one, I trust, will say that, save his own children, the Pharisees, if there be any of them left, which we will hope there are not. No! all these come from the gracious spirit of humanity—the spirit of Christ and of God. Pray to him, that he may take possession of all your thoughts, feelings, and desires, and purge you from every taint of selfishness. Give up your hearts to him; and grieve not, by any selfishness, passion, or hardness of your own, his gracious instructions: but let him teach you, and guide you, and purge you, and sanctify you, till you come to the stature of a perfect man, to the fulness of the measure of Christ, who could perfectly hate the sin, and yet perfectly love the sinner; who could see in every man, even in his enemies and murderers, a friend and a brother.

And you who are afflicted, remember, that if the spirit of humanity be the spirit of Christ, the spirit of Christ is also the spirit of humanity. What do I mean? This: that if that good Samaritan had Christ's spirit, was like Christ, then Christ has the same spirit, and is like that good Samaritan, utterly humane, for mere humanity's sake.

Yes, thou who art weary and heavy laden—thou who fanciest, at moments, that the Lord's arm is shortened, that it cannot save, and art ready to cry, My God, my God, why hast thou forsaken me?—take comfort, and look upon Christ. Thou wilt never be sure of the love of God, unless thou rememberest that it is the same as the love of Christ; and, by looking at Christ, learnest to know thy Father and his Father, whose likeness and image he is, and see that the spirit which proceeds alike from both of them is the spirit of humanity and love, which cannot help going forth to seek and to save thee, simply because thou art lost. Look, I say, at Christ, and be sure that what he bade the good Samaritan do to the wounded traveller, that same will he do to thee, because he is the Son of Man, human and humane.

Art thou robbed, wounded, deserted, left to die, worsted in the battle of life, and fallen in its rugged road, with no counsel, no strength, no hope, no purpose left? Then remember, that there is one walking to and fro in this world, unseen, but ever present, whose form is as the form of the Son of Man.

To him is given all power to execute judgment in heaven and earth, because he is the Son of Man. He is beholding the nations and fashioning all their hearts. Even as I speak now, he is pouring contempt on princes, and making the counsels of the people of no effect. Even now he is frustrating the tokens of the liars, and making diviners mad. He is smiting asunder mighty nations, and filling the lands with dead bodies. Even now he is coming, as he came of old from Bozra, treading down the people in his anger, and making them dumb in his fury; and their blood is sprinkled on his garments, and he hath stained all his raiment. For the day of vengeance is in his heart, and the year of his redeemed is come. He who ariseth terribly to shake the nations, has he time, has he will, to turn aside to attend to such as thee?

He has time, and he has will. No human being so mean, no human sorrow too petty, but what he has the time and the will, as well as the power, to have mercy on it, because he is the Son of Man. Therefore he will turn aside even to thee, whoever thou art, who art weary and heavy laden, and canst find no rest for thy soul, at the very moment, and in the very manner, which is best for thee. When thou hast suffered long enough, he will stablish, strengthen, settle thee. He will bind up thy wounds, and pour in the oil and the wine of his spirit—the Holy Ghost, the Comforter;

and will carry thee to his own inn, whereof it is written, He shall hide thee secretly in his own presence from the provoking of men; he shall keep thee in his tabernacle from the strife of tongues. He will give his servants charge over thee to keep thee in all thy ways; and when he comes again, he will repay them, and fetch thee away, to give thee rest in that eternal bosom of the Father, from which thou, like all human souls, camest forth at first, and to which thou shalt at last return, with all human souls who have in them that spirit of humanity, which is the spirit of God, and of Christ, and of eternal life.

SERMON XIV

CONSIDER THE LILIES OF THE FIELD.

(Preached on Easter Day, 1867.)

MATTHEW VI. 26, 28, 29.

Behold the fowls of the air : for they sow not, neither do they reap, nor gather into barns; yet your heavenly Father feedeth them. Are ye not much better than they? . . . And why take ye thought for raiment ? Consider the lilies of the field, how they grow; they toil not, neither do they spin : and yet I say unto you, That even Solomon in all his glory was not arrayed like one of these.

WHAT has this text to do with Easter-day? Let us think a while. Life and death; the battle between life and death; life conquered by death; and death conquered again by life. Those were the mysteries over which the men of old time thought, often till their hearts were sad.

They saw that they were alive; and they loved life, and would fain see good days. They saw, again, that they must die: but would death conquer life in them? Would they ever live again?

They saw that other things died, or seemed to die, and yet rose and lived again; and that gave them hope for themselves at times; but their hopes were very dim, till Christ came, and brought life and immortality to light.

They saw, I say, that other things died, or seemed to die, and yet lived again. Light rose out of darkness every morning and lived: but darkness, as they thought, killed the light at even, till it came to life again in the morning, and the sun rose once more. The sun himself—they thought of him as a glorious and life-giving being, who every morning fought his way up the sky, scattering the dark clouds with his golden arrows, and reigning for a-while in heaven, pouring down heat and growth and life: but he too must die. The dark clouds of evening must cover him. The red glare upon them was his dying blood. The twilight, which lingered after the sun was gone, was his bride, the dawn, come to soothe his dying hour. True, he had come to life again, often and often, morning after morning: but would it be so for ever? Would not a night come at last, after which he would never rise again? Would not he be worn out at last, and slain, in his long daily battle with the kingdom of darkness, which lay below the world; or with the dragon who tried to devour him, when the thunder clouds hid him from the sight, or the eclipse seemed to swallow him up before their eyes?

So, too, they felt about the seasons of the year. The winter came. The sun grew low and weak. Would he not die? The days grew short and dark. Would they not cease to be, and eternal night come on the earth? They had heard dimly of the dark northern land, where it was always winter, and the night was six months long. Why should it not be so in their own land in some evil time? Every autumn the rains and frost came on; the leaves fell; the flowers withered; the birds fled southward, or died of hunger and cold; the cattle starved in the field; the very men had much ado to live. Why should not winter conquer at last, and shut up the sun, the God of light and warmth and life, for ever in the place of darkness, cold, and death? So thought the old Syrians of Canaan, and taught the Jewish women to weep, as they themselves wept every autumn, over Adonai, the Lord, which was another name for the sun, slain, as they thought, by the winter cold and rain: and then, when spring-time came, with its sunshine, flowers, and birds, rejoiced that the sun had come to life again.

So thought the old Greeks, and told how Persephone, the fair maiden who was the spring-time, was stolen away by the king of darkness who lived beneath the earth; and how her mother earth would not be comforted for her loss, but sent barrenness on all the world till her daughter, the spring, was given back to her, to dwell for six months in the upper world of light, and six months in the darkness under ground.

So thought our old forefathers; and told

how Baldur (the Baal of the Bible), the god of light and heat, who was likewise the sun, was slain by treachery, and imprisoned for ever below in hell, the kingdom of darkness and of cold ; and how all things on earth, even the very trees and stones, wept for his death : yet all their tears could not bring back from death the god of life: nor any of the gods unlock the gates which held him in.

And because our forefathers were a sad and earnest folk ; because they lived in a sad and dreary climate, where winter was far longer and more bitter than it is, thank God, now ; therefore all their thoughts about winter and spring were sad ; and they grew to despair, at last, of life ever conquering death, or light conquering darkness. An age would come, they said, in which snow should fall from the four corners of the world, and the winters be three winters long; an evil age, of murder and adultery, and hatred between brethren, when all the ties of kin would be rent asunder, and wickedness should triumph on the earth.

Then should come that dark time which they called the twilight of the gods. Then the powers of evil would be let loose; the earth would go to ruin in darkness and in flame. All living things would die. The very gods would die, fighting to the last against the powers of evil, till the sun should sink for ever, and the world be a heap of ashes.

And then—so strangely does God's gift of hope linger in the hearts of men—they saw, beyond all that, a dim dream of a new heaven and a new earth in which should dwell righteousness; and of a new sun, more beautiful than ours; of a woman called "Life," hid safe while all the world around her was destroyed, fed on the morning dew, preserved to be the mother of a new and happier race of men. And so to them, heathens as they were, God whispered that Christ should some day bring life and immortality to light.

My friends, shall we sneer and laugh at all these dreams, as mere follies of the heathen? If we do so, we shall not show the spirit of God, or the mind of Christ. Nor shall we show our knowledge of the Bible. In it, the spirit of God, who inspired the Bible, does not laugh at these dreams. It rebukes them sternly whenever they are immoral, and lead men to do bad and foul deeds, as Ezekiel rebuked the Jewish women who wept for Thammuz, the dead summer. But that was because those Jewish women should have known better. They should have known—what the Old Testament tells us all through—what it was especially meant to tell the men who lived while it was being written, just because they had their fancies, and their fears about summer and winter, and life and death. And what ought they to have known? What does the Old Testament say? That life will conquer death, because God, the Lord Jehovah, even Jesus Christ, is Lord of heaven and earth. From the time that it was written in the Book of Genesis, that the Lord Jehovah said in his heart, ' I will not ' again curse the ground for man's sake: ' neither will I again smite any more any- ' thing living, as I have done, while the earth ' remaineth—seed time and harvest, and cold

'and heat, and summer and winter, and day
'and night, shall not cease'—from that time
the Jews were bound not to fear the powers
of nature, or the seasons, nor to fear for
them; for they were all in the government
of that one good God and Lord, who cared
for men, and loved them, and dealt justly by
them, and proved his love and justice by
bringing the children of Israel out of the land
of Egypt.

God treated these heathens, St. Paul says,
as we ought to treat our children. His wrath
was revealed from heaven against all ungodliness and unrighteousness of men. All wilful
disobedience and actual sin he punished, often
with terrible severity; but not their childish
mistakes and dreams about how this world
was made; just as we should not punish the
fancies of our children. The times of that
ignorance, says St. Paul, he winked at till
Christ came, and then he commanded all
men everywhere to repent, and believe in the
God who gave them rain and fruitful seasons,
filling their hearts with food and gladness.

For he had appointed a day in which he would judge the world in righteousness by that man whom he had ordained; of which he had given full assurance to all men, in that he had raised him from the dead.

Some, who were spoilt by false philosophy, mocked when they heard of the resurrection of the dead: but there were those who had kept something of the simple childlike faith of their forefathers, and who were prepared for the kingdom of God; and to them St. Paul's message came as an answer to the questions of their minds, and a satisfaction to the longings of their hearts.

The news of Christ,—of Christ raised from the dead to be the life and the light of the world,—stilled all their fears lest death should conquer life, and darkness conquer light.

So it was with all the heathen. So it was with our old forefathers, when they heard and believed the Gospel of Christ. They felt that (as St. Paul said) they were translated out of the kingdom of darkness into the kingdom of light, which was the kingdom of his dear Son; that now the world must look hopeful, cheerful to them; now they could live in hope of everlasting life; now they need sorrow no more for those who slept, as if they had no hope: for Christ had conquered death, and the evil spirit who had the power of death. Christ had harrowed hell, and burst the bonds of the graves. He, as man, and yet God, had been through the dark gate, and had returned through it in triumph, the first-born from the dead; and his resurrection was an everlasting sign and pledge that all who belonged to him should rise with him, and death be swallowed up in victory.

'So it pleased the Father,' says St. Paul, 'to gather together in Christ all things, 'whether in heaven or in earth.' In him were fulfilled, and more than fulfilled, the dim longings, the childlike dreams of heathen poets and sages, and of our own ancestors from whom we sprung. He is the desire of all nations; for whom all were longing, though they knew it not. He is the true sun; the sun of righteousness, who has arisen with healing on his wings, and translated us from the kingdom of darkness into the kingdom of light. He is the true Adonai, the Lord for whose death though we may mourn upon Good Friday, yet we rejoice this day for his resurrection. He is the true Baldur, the God of light and life, who, though he died by treachery, and descended into hell, yet needed not, to deliver him, the tears of all creation, of men or angels, or that any god should unlock for him the gates of death; for he rose by his own eternal spirit of light, and saith, 'I am 'he that was dead, and behold I am alive for 'evermore. Amen. And I have the keys of 'death and hell.'

And now we may see, it seems to me, what the text has to do with Easter-day. To my mind our Lord is using here the same parable which St. Paul preaches in his famous chapter which we read in the Burial Service. Be not anxious, says our Lord, for your life. Is not the life more than meat? There is an eternal life which depends not on earthly food, but on the will and word of God your Father; and that life in you will conquer death. Behold the birds of the air, which sow not, nor reap, nor gather into barns, to provide against the winter's need. But do they starve and die? Does not God guide them far away into foreign climes, and feed them there by his providence, and bring them back again in spring, as things alive from the dead? And can he not feed us (if it be his will) with a bread which comes down from heaven, and with every word which proceedeth out of the mouth of God?

Consider, again, the lilies of the field. We must take our Lord's words exactly. He is speaking of the lilies, the bulbous plants which spring into flower in countless thousands every spring, over the downs of Eastern lands. All the winter they are dead, unsightly roots, hidden in the earth. What can come of them? But no sooner does the sun of spring shine on their graves, than they rise into sudden life and beauty, as it pleases God, and every seed takes its own peculiar body Sown in corruption, they are raised in incorruption; sown in weakness, they are raised in power; sown in dishonour, they are raised in glory; delicate, beautiful in colour, perfuming the air with fragrance; types of immortality, fit for the crowns of angels. Consider the lilies of the field, how they grow. For even so is the resurrection of the dead.

Yes, not without a divine providence—yea, a divine inspiration—has this blessed Eastertide been fixed, by the Church of all ages, at the season when the earth shakes off her winter's sleep; when the birds come back and the flowers begin to bloom; when every seed which falls into the ground, and dies, and rises again with a new body, is a witness to us of the resurrection of Christ; and a witness, too, that we shall rise again; that in us, as in it, life shall conquer death: when every bird which comes back to sing and build among us, is a witness to us of the resurrection of Christ, and of our resurrection; and that in us, as in it, joy shall conquer sorrow.

The seed has passed through strange chances and dangers: of a thousand seeds shed in autumn, scarce one survives to grow in spring. Be it so. Still there is left, as Scripture says, a remnant, an elect, to rise again and live.

The birds likewise—they have been through strange chances, dangers, needs. Far away south to Africa they went—the younger ones by a way they had never travelled before. Thousands died in their passage south. Thousands more died in their passage back again this spring, by hunger and by storm. Be it so. Yet of them is left a seed, a remnant, an elect, and they are saved, to build once more in their old homes, and to rejoice in the spring, and pour out their songs to God who made them.

Some say that the seeds grow by laws of nature; the birds come back by instinct. Be it so. What Scripture says, and what we should believe, is this: that the seeds grow by the spirit of God, the Lord and Giver of life; that the birds come back, and sing, and build by the spirit of God, the Lord and Giver of life. He works not on them, things without reason, as he works on us reasonable souls: but he works on them nevertheless. They obey his call; they do his will; they show forth his glory; they return to life, they breed, they are preserved, by the same spirit by which the body of Jesus rose from the dead; and, therefore, every flower which blossoms, and every bird which sings, at Easter-tide; everything which, like the seeds, was dead, and is alive again, which, like the birds, was lost, and is found, is a type and token of Christ, their Maker, who was dead and is alive again; who was lost in hell on Easter-eve, and was found again in heaven for evermore; and the resurrection of the earth from her winter's sleep commemorates to us, as each blessed Easter-tide comes round, the resurrection of our Lord Jesus Christ, who made all the world, and redeemed all mankind, and sanctifieth to eternal life all the elect people of God: a witness to us that some day life shall conquer death, light conquer darkness, righteousness conquer sin, joy conquer grief; when the whole creation, which groaneth and travaileth in pain until now, shall have brought forth that of which it travails in labour; even the new heavens and the new earth, wherein shall be neither sighing nor sorrow, but God shall wipe away tears from all eyes.

SERMON XV.

THE JEWISH REBELLIONS.

1 Peter ii. 11.

Dearly beloved, I beseech you as strangers and pilgrims, abstain from fleshly lusts, which war against the soul.

I THINK that you will understand the text, and indeed the whole of St. Peter's first Epistle, better, if I explain to you somewhat the state of the Eastern countries of the world in St. Peter's time. The Romans, a short time before St. Peter was born, had conquered all the nations round them, and brought them under law and regular government. St. Peter now tells those to whom he wrote, that they must obey the Roman governors and their laws, for the Lord's sake. It was God's will and providence that the Romans should be masters of the world at that time. Jesus

Christ the Lord, the King of kings, had so ordained it in his inscrutable wisdom; and they must submit to it, not for fear of the Romans, but for the Lord's sake as the servants of God, who believed that he was governing the world by his Son Jesus Christ, and that he knew best how to govern it.

That was a hard lesson for them to learn; for they were Jews. This epistle, as the words of it show plainly, was written for Jews; both for those who believed in the Lord Jesus Christ as the true King of the Jews, and for those who ought to have believed in him, but did not. They were strangers and pilgrims (as St. Peter calls them), who had no city or government of their own, but had been scattered abroad among the Gentiles, and settled in all the great cities of the Roman Empire, especially in the East: in Babylon, from which St. Peter wrote his epistle, where the Jews had a great settlement in the rich plains of the river Euphrates; in Syria; in Asia Minor, which we now call Turkey in Asia: in Persia, and many other Eastern lands. There they lived by trade, very much as the Jews live among us now; and as long as they obeyed the Roman law, they were allowed to keep their own worship, and their own customs, and their law of Moses, and to have their synagogues in which they worshipped the true God every Sabbath-day. But evil times were coming on these prosperous Jews. Wicked emperors of Rome and profligate governors of provinces were about to persecute them. In Alexandria in Egypt, hundreds of them had been destroyed by lingering tortures, and thousands ruined and left homeless. Caligula, the mad emperor, had gone further still. Fancying himself a god, he had commanded that temples should be raised in his honour, and his statues worshipped everywhere. He had even gone so far as to command that his statue should be set up in the Temple of Jerusalem, and to do actually that which St. Paul prophesied a few years after the man of sin would do, 'Exalt 'himself over all that is called God, or that 'is worshipped; so that he would sit in the 'temple of God, and show himself as God.'

Then followed a strange scene, which will

help to explain much of this Epistle of St. Peter. The Jews of Jerusalem did not rise in rebellion. They did what St. Peter told the Jews of Asia Minor to do. They determined to suffer for well-doing,—to die as martyrs, not as rebels. Petronius, the Roman governor who was sent to carry out the order, was a strange mixture of good and bad. He was a peculiarly profligate and luxurious man. He wrote one of the foulest books which ever disgraced the pen of man But he was kind-hearted, humane, rational. He had orders to set up the Emperor's statue in the temple at Jerusalem; and no doubt he laughed inwardly at the folly: but he must obey orders. Yet he hesitated, when he landed and saw the Jews come to him in thousands, covering the country like a cloud, young and old, rich and poor, unarmed, many clothed in sackcloth and with ashes on their heads, and beseeching him that he would not commit this abomination. He rebuked them sternly. He had a whole army at his back, and would compel them to obey. They answered that they must obey God rather than man. Petronius's heart relented; he left his soldiers behind; and went on to try the Jews at Tiberias. There he met a similar band. He tried again to be stern with them. All other nations had worshipped the Emperor's image, why should not they? Would they make war against their emperor? 'We have no thought of war,' they cried with one voice, ' but we will submit to be massacred rather ' than break our law;' and at once the whole crowd fell with their faces to the earth, and declared that they were ready to offer their throats to the swords of the Roman soldiers.

For forty days that scene lasted; it was the time for sowing, and the whole land lay untilled. Petronius could do nothing with people who were ready to be martyrs, but not rebels; and he gave way. He excused himself to the mad emperor as he best could. He promised the Jews that he would do all he could for them, even at the risk of his own life—and he very nearly lost his life in trying to save them. But the thing tided over, and the poor Jews conquered, as the Christian martyrs conquered afterwards, by resignation; by that highest courage which shows itself not in anger but in patience, and suffering instead of rebelling.

Well it had been for the Jews elsewhere if they had been of the same mind. But near Babylon, just about the time St. Peter wrote his epistle, the Jews broke out in open rebellion. Two Jewish orphans, who had been bred as weavers and ran away from a cruel master, escaped into the marshes, and there became the leaders of a great band of robbers. They defeated the governor of Babylon in battle; they went to the court of the heathen king of Persia, and became great men there. One of them had the other poisoned, and then committed great crimes, wasted the country of Babylon with fire and sword, and came to a miserable end, being slaughtered in bed when in a drunken sleep. Then the Babylonians rose on all the Jews and massacred them: the survivors fled to the great city of Seleucia, and mixed themselves up in party riots with the heathens; the heathens turned on them and slew 50,000 of them; and so, as St. Peter told them, judgment began at the house of God.

Whether this massacre of the Babylonian Jews happened just before or just after St. Peter wrote his epistle from Babylon, we cannot tell. But it is plain, I think, that either this matter or what led to it was in his mind. It seems most likely that it had happened a little before, and that he wrote to the Jews in the north-east of Asia Minor, to warn them against giving way to the same lawless passions which had brought ruin and misery on the Jews of Babylon.

For they were in great danger of falling into the same misery and ruin. The Romans expected the Jews to rebel all over the world. And, as it fell out, they did rebel, and perished in vast numbers miserably, because they would not take St. Peter's advice; because they would not obey every ordinance of man for the Lord's sake; because they would not honour all men: but looked on all men as the enemies of God.

Good for them it would have been, had they taken St. Peter's advice, which was the only plan, he said, to save their souls and lives in those terrible times. Good for them if they had believed St. Peter's gospel, when he told them that God had chosen them to obedience, and purification by the blood of Christ, to an inheritance undefiled and that faded not away.

He said that, remember, to all the Jews, whether Christians or not. St. Peter took for granted that Christ was Lord and King of all the Jews, whether they believed it or not. He did not say, 'If you believe in Christ, then he is your King; if not, then he is not;' but—Because you are Jews, you are all Christ's subjects; to him you owe faith, loyalty, and obedience. It was of him the old Jewish prophets foretold, and saw that their prophecies of Christ's coming would be fulfilled, not in their own time, but in your time—in the time of the Jews to whom he spoke. Therefore they were to give up the foolish practices which had been handed down to them from their forefathers. Therefore they were to give up fleshly lusts, which warred against the soul, and would only bring them to destruction; therefore they were to be holy, even as God was holy; therefore they were to purify their souls in sincere brotherly love; therefore they were to keep their conduct honourable among the Gentiles, that, though they were now spoken against as evil-doers, they might see their good works, and glorify God in the coming day of visitation. Therefore they were to submit to every ordinance of man for the Lord's sake; and trust to Christ, their true King in heaven, to deliver them from oppression, and free them from injustice, in his own good way and time. Free men they were in the sight of God, and unjustly enslaved by the Romans: but they were not to make their being free men a cloak and excuse for malice and evil passions against the Gentiles (as too many of the Jews were doing), but remember that they were the servants of God; and serve him, and trust in him to deliver them in his own way and time, by his Son Jesus Christ.

Those Jews who believed St. Peter's gospel and good news that Christ was their King and Saviour, kept their souls in peace.

Those Jews who did not believe St. Peter—and they, unhappily for them, were the far greater number—broke out into mad rebellion again, and perished in vast numbers, till they were destroyed off the face of the earth (as St. Peter had warned them) by their own fleshly lusts, which warred against the soul.

But what has this to do with us?

It has everything to do with us, if we believe that we are Christian men; that Christ is our King, and the King of all the world, just as much as he was King of the Jews; that all power is given to him in heaven and earth, and that he is actually exercising his power, and governing all heaven and earth.

Yes. If we really believed in the kingdom of God and Christ; if we really believed that the fate of nations is determined, not by kings, not by conquerors, not by statesmen, not by parliaments, not by the people, but by God; that we, England, the world, are going God's way, and not our own: then we should look hopefully, peacefully, contentedly, on the matters which are too apt now to fret us; for we should say more often than we do, 'It is 'the Lord: let him do what seemeth to him 'good.'

When we see new opinions taking hold of men's minds; when we see great changes becoming certain; then, instead of being angry and terrified, we should say with Gamaliel the wise, 'Let them alone: if this counsel or this 'work be of men, it will come to nought; if 'it be of God, you cannot overthrow it, lest 'haply you be found fighting against God.' If, again, we fancied ourselves aggrieved by any law, we should not say, 'It is unjust, therefore I will not obey it:' for it would seem a small matter to us whether the law was unjust to us, which only means, in most cases, that the law is hard on us personally, and that we do not like it; for almost every one considers things just which make for his own interest, while whatever is against his interest is of course unjust. We should say, 'Let the 'law be hard on me, yet I will obey it for the 'Lord's sake; if it can be altered by fair and

'lawful means, well and good; but if not, I
'will take it as one more burden which I am
'to bear patiently for the sake of him who
'lays it on me, Christ my Lord and my King.'

The true question with us ought to be, Does the law force us to do that which is wrong?

If so, we are bound not to obey it, as the Jews were bound not to obey the law which commanded Cæsar's image to be set up in the Temple. But if any man knows of a law in this land which compels him to do a wrong thing, I know of none. And let no man fancy that such submission shows a slavish spirit. Not so. St. Peter did not wish to encourage a slavish spirit in Jews and Christians. He told them that they were free: but that they were not to use that belief as a cloak of maliciousness—of spiteful, bitter, and turbulent conduct. And as a fact, those who have done most for true freedom, in all ages, have not been the violent, noisy, bitter, rebellious spirits, who have cried, 'We are the masters, who shall rule over us?' but the God-fearing, patient, law-abiding men, who would obey every ordinance of man for the Lord's sake, whether it seemed to them altogether just or not, unless they saw it was ruinous not to themselves merely, but to their country, and to their children after them.

It is because men in their own minds do not believe that Christ is the ruler of the world, that they lose all hope of God's delivering them, and break out into mad rebellion. It is because, again, men do not believe that Christ is the ruler of the world, that, when their rebellion has failed, they sink into slavishness and dull despair, and bow their necks to the yoke of the first tyrant who arises; and try to make a covenant with death and hell. Better far for them, had they made a covenant with Christ, who is ready to deliver men from death and hell in this world, as well as in the world to come.

But he who believes in Christ, in the living Christ, the ordering Christ, the governing Christ, will possess his soul in patience. He will not fret himself, lest he should do evil; because he can always put his trust in the Lord, until the tyranny be overpast. He will not hastily rebel: but neither will he truckle basely and cowardly to the ways of this wicked world. For Christ the Lord hates those ways, and has judged them, and doomed them to destruction; and he reigns, and will reign, till he hath put all enemies under his feet.

SERMON XVI.

TERROR BY NIGHT.

(*Preached in Lent.*)

PSALM XCI. 5.

Thou shalt not be afraid for the terror by night.

YOU may see, if you will read your Bible, that the night is spoken of in the Old Testament much as we speak of it now, as a beautiful and holy thing. The old Jews were not afraid of any terror by night. They rejoiced to consider the heavens, the work of God's fingers, the moon and the stars, which he had ordained. They looked on night, as we do, as a blessed time of rest and peace for men, in which the beasts of the forest seek their meat from God, while all things are springing and growing, man knows not how, under the sleepless eye of a good and loving Creator.

But, on the other hand, you may remark that St. Paul, in his Epistles, speaks of night in a very different tone. He is always opposing night to day, and darkness to light; as if darkness was evil in itself, and a pattern of all evil in men's souls. And St. Paul knew what he was saying, and knew how to say it; for he spoke by the Holy Spirit of God.

The reason of this difference is simple. The old Jews spoke of God's night, such as we country folks may see, thank God, as often as we will. St. Paul spoke of man's night, such as it might be seen, alas! in the cities of the Roman empire. All those to whom he wrote—Romans, Corinthians, Ephesians, and the rest—dwelt in great cities, heathen and profligate; and night in them was mixed up with all that was ugly, dangerous, and foul. They were bad enough by day: after sunset, they became hells on earth. The people, high and low, were sunk in wickedness; the lower classes in poverty, and often despair. The streets were utterly unlighted; and in the darkness robbery, housebreaking, murder, were so common, that no one who had anything to lose went through the streets without his weapon or a guard; while inside the houses, things went on at night—works of darkness—of which no man who knows of them dare talk. For as St. Paul says, 'It is a shame even to speak of 'those things which are done by them in 'secret.' Evil things are done by night still, in London, Paris, New York, and many a great city; but they are pure, respectable, comfortable, and happy, when compared with one of those old heathen cities, which St. Paul knew but too well.

Again. Our own forefathers were afraid of the night and its terrors, and looked on night as on an ugly time: but for very different reasons from those for which St. Paul warned his disciples of night and the works of darkness. Though they lived in the country, they did not rejoice in God's heaven, or in the moon and stars which he had ordained. They fancied that the night was the time in which all ghastly and ugly phantoms began to move; that it was peopled with ghosts, skeletons, demons, witches, who held revels on the hill-tops, or stole into houses to suck the life out of sleeping men. The cry of the wild fowl, and the howling of the wind, were to them the yells of evil spirits. They dared not pass a graveyard by night for fear of seeing things of which we will not talk. They fancied that the forests, the fens, the caves, were full of spiteful and ugly spirits, who tempted men to danger and to death; and when they prayed to be delivered from the perils and dangers of the night, they prayed not only against those real dangers of fire, of robbers, of sudden sickness, and so forth, against which we all must pray, but against a thousand horrible creatures which the good God never created, but which their own fancy had invented.

Now in the Bible, from beginning to end, you will find no teaching of this kind. That there are angels, and that there are also evil spirits, the Bible says distinctly; and that they can sometimes appear to men. But it is most worthy of remark how little the Bible says about them, not how much; how it keeps them, as it were, in the background, instead of bringing them forward; while our forefathers seem continually talking of them, continually bringing them forward—I had almost said they thought of nothing else. If you compare the Holy Bible with the works which were most popular among our forefathers, especially among the lower class, till within the last 200 years, you will see at once what I mean,—how ghosts, apparitions, demons, witchcraft, are perpetually spoken of in them; how seldom they are spoken of in the Bible; lest, I suppose, men should think of them rather than of God, as our forefathers seem to have been but too much given to do.

And so with this Psalm. It takes for granted that men will have terrors by night; that they will be at times afraid of what may come to them in the darkness. But it tells them not to be afraid, for that as long as they say to God, 'Thou art my hope and my stronghold; in thee will I trust,' so long they will not be afraid for any terror by night.

It was because our forefathers did not say

that, that they were afraid, and the terror by night grew on them; till at times it made them half mad with fear of ghosts, witches, demons, and such-like; and with the madness of fear came the madness of cruelty; and they committed, again and again, such atrocities as I will not speak of here; crimes for which we must trust that God has forgiven them, for they knew not what they did.

But, though we happily no longer believe in the terror by night which comes from witches, demons, or ghosts, there is another kind of terror by night in which we must believe, for it comes to us from God, and should be listened to as the voice of God: even that terror about our own sinfulness, folly, weakness which comes to us in dreams or in sleepless nights. Some will say, 'These painful 'dreams, these painful waking thoughts, are 'merely bodily, and can be explained by 'bodily causes, known to physicians.' Whether they can or not, matters very little to you and me. Things may be bodily, and yet teach us spiritual lessons. A book—the very Bible itself—is a bodily thing: bodily leaves of paper, printed with bodily ink; and yet out of it we may learn lessons for our souls of the most awful and eternal importance. And so with these night fancies and night thoughts. We may learn from them. We are forced often to learn from them, whether we will or not. They are often God's message to us, calling us to repentance and amendment of life. They are often God's book of judgment, wherein our sins are written, which God is setting before us, and showing us the things which we have done.

Who that has come to middle age does not know how dreams sometimes remind him painfully of what he once was, of what he would be still, without God's grace? How in his dreams he finds himself tempted by the old sins; giving way to the old meannesses, weaknesses, follies? How dreams remind him, awfully enough, that though his circumstances have changed,—his opinions, his whole manner of life, have changed—yet he is still the same person that he was ten, twenty, thirty, forty years ago, and will be for ever? Nothing bears witness to the abiding, enduring, immortal oneness of the soul like dreams when they prove to a man, in a way which cannot be mistaken—that is, by making him do the deed over again in fancy—that he is the same person who told that lie, felt that hatred, many a year ago; and who would do the same again, if God's grace left him to that weak and sinful nature, which is his master in sleep, and runs riot in his dreams. Whether God sends to men in these days dreams which enable them to look forward, and to foretell things to come, I cannot say. But this I can say, that God sends dreams to men which enable them to look back, and recollect things past, which they had forgotten only too easily; and that these humbling and penitential dreams are God's warning that (as the Article says) the infection of nature doth remain, even in those who are regenerate; that nothing but the continual help of God's Spirit will keep us from falling back, or falling away.

Again: those sad thoughts which weigh on the mind when lying awake at night, when all things look black to a man; when he is more ashamed of himself, more angry with himself, more ready to take the darkest view of his own character and of his own prospects of life, than he ever is by day,—do not these thoughts, too, come from God? Is it not God who is holding the man's eyes waking? Is it not God who is making him search out his own heart, and commune with his spirit? I believe that so it is. If any one says, 'It is all caused by the darkness and 'silence. You have nothing to distract your 'attention as you have by day, and therefore 'the mind becomes unwholesomely excited, 'and feeds upon itself,' I answer, then they are good things, now and then, this darkness and this silence, if they do prevent the mind from being distracted, as it is all day long, by business and pleasure; if they leave a man's soul alone with itself, to look itself in the face, and be thoroughly ashamed of what it sees. In the noise and glare of the day, we are all too apt to fancy that all is right with us, and say, 'I am rich, and increased with goods, and have need of nothing;' and the night does us a kindly office if it helps us to find out that we knew not that we were poor, and miserable, and blind, and naked—not only in the sight of God, but in our own sight, when we look honestly at ourselves.

The wise man says:—

> 'Oh, would some power the gift but give us,
> To see ourselves as others see us!'

and those painful thoughts make us do that. For if we see some faults in ourselves, be sure our neighbours see them likewise, and perhaps many more beside.

But more: these sad thoughts make us see ourselves as God sees us. For if we see faults in ourselves, we may be sure that the pure and holy God, in whose sight the very heavens are not clean, and who charges his angels with folly, sees our faults with infinitely greater clearness, and in infinitely greater number. So let us face those sad night thoughts, however painful, however humiliating they may be; for by them God is calling us to repentance, and forcing us to keep Lent in spirit and in truth, whether we keep it outwardly or not.

'What,' some may say, 'you would have us, then, afraid of the terror by night?' My dear friends, that is exactly what I would not have. I would teach you from Holy Scripture how to profit by the terror, how to thank God for the terror, instead of being afraid of it, as you otherwise certainly will be. For these ugly dreams, these sad thoughts do come, whether you choose or not. Whether you choose or not, you all have, or will have seasons of depression, of anxiety, of melancholy. Shall they teach you, or merely terrify you? Shall they only bring remorse, or shall they bring repentance?

Remorse. In that is nothing but pain. A man may see all the wrong and folly he has done; he may fret over it; torment himself with it, curse himself for it, and yet be the worse, and not the better, for what he sees. If he be a strong-minded man, he may escape from remorse in the bustle of business or pleasure. If he be a weak-minded man, he may escape from it in drunkenness, as hundreds do; or he may fall into melancholy, superstition, despair, suicide.

But if his sadness breeds, not remorse, but repentance—that is, in one word, if, instead of keeping his sins to himself, he takes his sins to God—then all will be well. Then he will not be afraid of the terror, but thankful for it, when he knows that it is what St. Paul calls, the terror of the Lord.

This is why the old Psalmists were not afraid of the terror by night; because they knew that their anxiety had come from God, and therefore went to God for forgiveness, for help, for comfort. Therefore it is that one says, 'I am weary of groaning. Every night 'wash I my bed, and water my couch with 'my tears,' and yet says the next moment, 'Away from me, all ye that work vanity. 'The Lord hath heard the voice of my weep- 'ing. The Lord will receive my prayer.'

Therefore it is that another says, 'While I 'held my sins my bones waxed old through 'my daily complaining;' and the next moment—'I said I will confess my sins unto the 'Lord, and so thou forgavest the wickedness 'of my sin.'

Therefore it is that again another says,

'Thou holdest mine eyes waking. I am so
'feeble that I cannot speak. I call to re-
'membrance my sin, and in the night season
'I commune with my heart, and search out
'my spirit. Will the Lord absent himself
'for ever, and will he be no more entreated?
'Is his mercy clean gone for ever, and his
'promise come utterly to an end for ever-
'more? And I said, It is mine own infirmity;
'but I will remember the years of the right
'hand of the most Highest. I will remember
'the works of the Lord, and call to mind the
'wonders of old.'

And another, 'Why art thou so heavy, O
'my soul, and why art thou so disquieted
'within me? O put thy trust in God, for I
'shall yet give him thanks, who is the help
'of my countenance, and my God.'

And therefore it is, that our Lord Jesus Christ, in order that he might taste sorrow for every man, and be made in all things like to his brethren, endured, once and for all, in the garden of Gethsemane, the terror which cometh by night, as none ever endured it before or since; the agony of dread, the agony of helplessness, in which he prayed yet more earnestly, and his sweat was as great drops of blood falling down to the ground. And there appeared an angel from heaven strengthening him; because he stood not on his own strength, but cast himself on his Father and our Father, on his God and our God. So says St. Paul, who tells us how our Lord, in the days of his flesh, when he had offered up prayers and supplications, with strong crying and tears, unto him that was able to save him from death, and was heard in that he feared—though he were a son, yet learned he obedience by the things which he suffered; and being made perfect, he became the Author of everlasting salvation unto all them that obey him.

Oh, may we all, in the hour of shame and sadness, in the hour of darkness and confusion, and, above all, in the hour of death and the day of judgment, take refuge with him in whom alone is help, and comfort, and salvation for this life and the life to come— even Jesus Christ, who died for us on the cross.

SERMON XVII.

THE SON OF THUNDER.

St. John i. 1.

In the beginning was the Word, and the Word was with God, and the Word was God.

WE read this morning the first chapter of the Gospel according to St. John.

Some of you, I am sure, must have felt, as you heard it, how grand was the very sound of the words. Some one once compared the sound of St. John's Gospel to a great church bell: simple, slow, and awful; and awful just because it is so simple and slow. The words are very short,—most of them of one syllable, —so that even a child may understand them if he will: but every word is full of meaning.

'In the beginning was the Word, and the Word was with God, and the Word was

'God. The same was in the beginning with
'God. All things were made by him; and
'without him was not anything made that
'was made. In him was life; and the life
'was the light of men. And the light shineth
'in darkness; and the darkness comprehended
it not.'

Those, I hold, are perhaps the deepest words ever written by man. Whole books have been written, and whole books more might be written upon them, and on the words which come after them. 'That was
'the true Light, which lighteth every man
'that cometh into the world. He was in the
'world, and the world was made by him, and
'the world knew him not. He came unto his
'own, and his own received him not. But
'as many as received him, to them gave he
'power to become the sons of God, even to
'them that believe on his name: which were
'born, not of blood, nor of the will of the
'flesh, nor of the will of man, but of God.
'And the Word was made flesh, and dwelt
'among us (and we beheld his glory, the
'glory as of the only-begotten of the Father),

'full of grace and truth.' They go down to the mystery of all mysteries,—to the mystery of the unfathomable One God, who dwells alone in the light which none can approach unto, self-sustained and self-sufficing for ever. And then they go on to the other great mystery—how that God comes forth out of himself to give life and light to all things which he has made; and what is the bond between the Abysmal Father in heaven, and us his human children, and the world in which we live:—even Jesus Christ, God of the substance of his Father, begotten before the worlds, and man of the substance of his mother, born in the world.

Yes. The root and ground of all true philosophy lies in this chapter. Its words are so deep that the wisest man might spend his life over them without finding out all that they mean. And yet they are so simple that any child can understand enough of their meaning to know its duty, and to do it.

Remark, again, how short the sentences are. Each is made up of a very few words, and followed by a full stop, that our minds may come to a full stop likewise, and think over what we have heard before St. John goes on to tell us more.

Yes. St. John does not hurry either himself or us. He takes his time; and he wishes us to take our time likewise. His message will keep; for it is eternal. It is not a story of yesterday, or to-day, or to-morrow. It is the story of eternity,—of what is, and was, and always will be.

Always has the Word been with God, and always will he be God.

Always has the Word been making all things, and always will he be making.

Always has the Spirit been proceeding, and always will the Spirit be proceeding, from the Word and from the Father of the Word, giving their light and their life to men.

St. John's message will last for ever; and therefore he tells it slowly and deliberately, knowing that no time can change what he has to say; for it is the good news of the Word, Jesus Christ, who is the same yesterday, to-day, and for ever, because he is God of very God, eternally in the bosom of the Father.

Now St. John, who writes thus simply and quietly, was no weak or soft person. He was one of the two whom the Lord surnamed Boanerges, the Son of Thunder—the man of the loud and awful voice. Painters have liked to draw St. John as young, soft, and feminine, because he was the Apostle of Love. I beg you to put that sentimental notion out of your minds, and to remember that the only hint which Holy Scripture gives us about St. John's person is, that he was 'a Son of Thunder;' that his very voice, when he chose, was awful; that he, and his brother James, before they were converted, were not of a soft, but of a terrible temper; that it was James and John, the Sons of Thunder, who wanted to call down thunder and lightning from heaven on all the villages who would not receive the Lord.

A Son of Thunder. Think over that name, and think over it carefully, remembering that it was our Lord himself who gave St. John the name; and that it therefore has, surely, some deep meaning.

Do not fancy that it means merely a loud and noisy person. I have known too many, carelessly looking only at the outsides and shows of things, and not at their inside and reality, fancy that that was what it meant. I have known them fancy that they themselves were sons of thunder when they raved and shouted, and used violent language, in preaching, or in public speaking. And I have heard foolish people honour such men the more, and think them the more in earnest, the more noise they made, and say of him, 'He is a 'true Boanerges—a Son of Thunder, like 'St. John.'

Like St. John? The only sermon of St. John's which we have on record is that which they say he used to preach over and over again when he was carried as an old man into his church at Ephesus. And that was no more than these few words over and over again, Sunday after Sunday, 'Little children, love one another.'

That was the way in which St. John, the

Son of Thunder, spoke when age and long obedience to the Spirit of God had taught him how to use his strength wisely and well.

Like St. John? Is there anywhere, in St. John's Gospel or Epistles, one violent expression? One sentence of great swelling words? Are not the words of the Son of Thunder, as I have been telling you, peculiarly calm, slow, simple, gentle? Can those whose mouths are full of noisy and violent talk, be true Sons of Thunder, if St. John was one?

No. And if you will think for yourselves, you will see that there is a deeper meaning in our Lord's name for St. John than merely that he was a loud and violent man.

You hear the roar of the thunder, but you know surely that it is not the thunder itself; that it is only its echo rolling on from cloud to cloud and hill from hill.

But the thunder itself—if you have ever been close enough to it to hear it—is very different from that, and far more awful. Still and silently it broods till its time is come. And then there is one ear-piercing crack, one blinding flash, and all is over. Nothing so swift, so instantaneous, as the thunder itself, and yet nothing so strong.

And such are those sudden flashes of indignation against sin and falsehood which break out for a moment in St. John's writing, piercing, like the Word of God himself, the very joints and marrow of the heart, and showing, in one terrible word, what is the real matter with the bad man's soul; as the thunderbolt lights up for an instant the whole heavens far and wide. 'If we say that we 'have fellowship with God, and walk in dark- 'ness, we lie.' In that one plain, ugly word, he tells us the whole truth, frightful as it is, and then he goes on calmly once more. And again:

'He that saith, I know God, and keepeth 'not his commandments, is a liar. He that 'committeth sin is of the devil. He that 'hateth his brother is a murderer. If a man 'say, I love God, and hateth his brother, he 'is a liar; for he that loveth not his brother 'whom he hath seen, how can he love God whom he hath not seen? He that doeth

'good is of God; but he that doeth evil has
'not seen God.'

Such words as these, coming as they do amid the usually quiet and gentle language of St. John—these are truly words of thunder; going straight to their mark, tearing off the mask from hypocrisy and self-deceiving and false religion, and speaking the truth in majesty.

And yet there is no noisiness, no wordiness, about them; nothing like rant or violence. Such a man is a liar, says St. John: but he says no more. That is all, and that is enough.

So speaks the true Son of Thunder. And his words, like the thunder, echo from land to land; and we hear them now, this day, in a foreign tongue, eighteen hundred years after they were written: while thousands of bigger noisier, and frothier words and more violent books have been lost and forgotten utterly.

And now, my friends, we may find in St. John's example a wholesome lesson for ourselves. We may learn from it that noisiness is not earnestness, that violence is not strength. Noise is a sign of want of faith, and violence is a sign of weakness.

The man who is really in earnest, who has real faith in what he is saying and doing, will not be noisy, and loud, and in a hurry, as it is written, 'He that believeth will not make haste.' He that is really strong; he who knows that he can do his work, if he takes his time and uses his wit, and God prospers him—he will not be violent, but will work on in silence and peaceful industry, as it is written, 'Thy strength is to sit still.'

I know that you here do not require this warning much for yourselves. There is, thank God, something in our quiet, industrious, country life which breeds in men that solid, sober temper, the temper which produces much work and little talk, which is the mark of a true Englishman, a true gentleman, and a true Christian.

But if you go (as more and more of you will go) into the great towns, you will hear much noisy and violent speaking from pulpits, and at public meetings. You will read much noisy and violent writing in newspapers and books.

Now I say to you, distrust such talk. It may seem to you very earnest and passionate. Distrust it for that very reason. It may seem to you very eloquent and full of fine words. Distrust it for that very reason. The man who cannot tell his story without wrapping it up in fine words, generally does not know very clearly what he is talking about. The man who cannot speak or write without scolding and exaggeration, is not very likely to be able to give sound advice to his fellow-men.

Remember that it is by violent language of this kind, in all ages, that fanatical preachers have deceived silly men and women to their shame and ruin; and mob-leaders have stirred up riots and horrible confusions. Remember this: and distrust violent and wordy persons wheresoever you shall meet them : but after listening to them, if you must, go home, and take out your Bibles, and read the Gospel of St. John, and see how he spoke, the true Son of Thunder, whose words are gone out into all lands, and their sound unto the end of the world, just because they are calm and sober, plain and simple, like the words of Jesus Christ his Lord and our Lord, who spake as never man spake.

And for ourselves—let us remember our Lord's own warning: 'Let your Yea be Yea, 'and your Nay Nay; for whatsoever is more 'than these cometh of evil.'

Tell your story plainly and calmly; speak your mind if you must. But speak it quietly. Do not try to make out the worst case for your adversary; do not exaggerate; do not use strong language: say the truth, the whole truth; but say nothing but the truth, in patience and in charity. For everything beyond that comes of evil,—of some evil or fault in us. Either we are not quite sure that we are right; or we have lost our temper, and then we see the whole matter awry, through the mist of passion; or we are selfish, and looking out for our own interest, or our own credit, instead of judging the matter fairly. This, or something else, is certainly wrong in us whenever we give way to violent language.

Therefore, whenever we are tempted to say more than is needful, let us remember St. John's words, and ask God for his Holy Spirit, the spirit of love, which, instead of weakening a man's words, makes them all the stronger in the cause of truth, because they are spoken in love.

SERMON XVIII.

HUMILITY.

Luke v. 8.

Depart from me; for I am a sinful man, O Lord.

FEW stories in the New Testament are as well known as this. Few go home more deeply to the heart of man. Most simple, most graceful is the story, and yet it has in it depths unfathomable.

Great painters have loved to draw, great poets have loved to sing, that scene on the lake of Gennesaret. The clear blue water, land-locked with mountains; the meadows on the shore, gay with their lilies of the field, on which our Lord bade them look, and know the bounty of their Father in heaven;

the rich gardens, olive-yards, and vineyards on the slopes; the towns and villas scattered along the shore, all of bright white limestone, gay in the sun; the crowds of boats, fishing continually for the fish which swarm to this day in the lake;—everywhere beautiful country life, busy and gay, healthy and civilized likewise—and in the midst of it, the Maker of all heaven and earth sitting in a poor fisher's boat, and condescending to tell them where the shoal of fish was lying. It is a wonderful scene. Let us thank God that it happened once on earth. Let us try to see what we may learn from it in these days, in which our God and Saviour no longer walks this earth in human form.

'Ah!' some may say, 'but for that very 'reason there is no lesson in the story for 'us in these days. True it is, that God does 'not walk the earth now in human form. 'He works no miracles, either for fishermen, 'or for any other men. We shall never see 'a miraculous draught of fishes. We shall 'never be convinced, as St. Peter was, by a 'miracle, that Christ is close to us. What has the story to do with us?'

My friends, are things, after all, so different now from what they were then? Is our case after all so very different from St. Peter's? God and Christ cannot change, for they are eternal—the same yesterday, to-day, and for ever; and if Christ was near St. Peter on the lake of Gennesaret, he is near us now, and here; for in him we live and move and have our being; and he is about our path, and about our bed, and spieth out all our ways: near us for ever, whether we know it or not. And human nature cannot change. There is in us the same heart as there was in St. Peter, for evil and for good. When St. Peter found suddenly that it was the Lord who was in his boat, his first feeling was one of fear: 'Depart from me; for I am a sinful man, O Lord.' And when we recollect at moments that God is close to us, watching all we do, all we say, yea, all we think, are we not afraid, for the moment at least? Do we not feel the thought of God's presence a burden? Do we never long to hide from God?—to forget God again, and cry in our hearts: 'Depart from me; for I am a sinful man, O Lord'?

God grant to us all, that after that first feeling of dread and awe is over, we may go on, as St. Peter went on, to the better feelings of admiration, loyalty, worship; and say at last, as St. Peter said afterwards, when the Lord asked him if he too would leave him: 'Lord, to whom shall we go? for thou hast the words of eternal life.'

But do I blame St. Peter for saying, 'De-'part from me; for I am a sinful man, O 'Lord'? God forbid! Who am I, to blame St. Peter? Especially when even the Lord Jesus did not blame him, but only bade him not to be afraid.

And why did the Lord not blame him, even when he asked Him to go away?

Because St. Peter was honest. He said frankly and naturally what was in his heart. And honesty, even if it is mistaken, never offends God, and ought never to offend men. God requires truth in the inward parts; and if a man speaks the truth—if he expresses his own thoughts and feelings frankly and honestly—then, even if he is not right, he is at least on the only road to get right, as St. Peter was.

He spoke not from dislike of our Lord, but from modesty; from a feeling of awe, of uneasiness, of dread, at the presence of one who was infinitely greater, wiser, better than himself.

And that feeling of reverence and modesty, even when it takes the shape, as it often will in young people, of shyness and fear, is a divine and noble feeling—the beginning of all goodness. Indeed, I question whether there can be any real and sound goodness in any man's heart, if he has no modesty, and no reverence. Boldness, forwardness, self-conceit, above all in the young—we know how ugly they are in our eyes; and the Bible tells us again and again how ugly they are in the sight of God.

The truly great and free and noble soul —and St. Peter's soul was such—is that of the man who feels awe and reverence in the presence of those who are wiser and holier than himself; who is abashed and humbled when he compares himself with his betters, just because his standard is so high. Because he knows how much better he should be than he is; because he is discontented with himself, ashamed of himself, therefore he shrinks, at first, from the very company which, after a while, he learns to like best, because it teaches him most. And so it was with St. Peter's noble soul. He felt himself, in the presence of that pure Christ, a sinful man:—not perhaps what we should call sinful; but sinful in comparison of Christ. He felt his own meanness, ignorance, selfishness, weakness. He felt unworthy to be in such good company. He felt unworthy,—he, the ignorant fisherman,—to have such a guest in his poor boat. 'Go elsewhere, Lord,' he tried to say, 'to a place and to companions more 'fit for thee. I am ashamed to stand in 'thy presence. I am dazzled by the bright-'ness of thy countenance, crushed down by 'the thought of thy wisdom and power, 'uneasy lest I say or do something unfit 'for thee; lest I anger thee unawares in my 'ignorance, clumsiness; lest I betray to thee 'my own bad habits: and those bad habits 'I feel in thy presence as I never felt before. 'Thou art too condescending; thou honourest 'me too much; thou hast taken me for a 'better man than I am; thou knowest not 'what a poor miserable creature I am at 'heart—"Depart from me; for I am a sinful 'man, O Lord."'

There spoke out the truly noble soul, who was ready the next moment, as soon as he had recovered himself, to leave all and follow Christ; who was ready afterwards to wander, to suffer, to die upon the cross for his Lord; and who, when he was led out to execution, asked to be crucified (as it is said St. Peter actually did) with his head downwards; for it was too much honour for him to die looking up to heaven, as his Lord had died.

Do you not understand me yet? Then think what you would have thought of St. Peter, if, instead of saying, 'Depart from me; for I am a sinful man, O Lord,' St. Peter had

said, 'Stay with me, for I am a holy man, O
'Lord. I am just the sort of person who
'deserves the honour of thy company; and
'my boat, poor though it is, more fit for
'thee than the palace of a king.' Would
St. Peter have seemed to you then wiser or
more foolish, better or worse, than he does
now, when in his confused honest humility,
he begs the Lord to go away and leave him?
And do you not feel that a man is (as a
great poet says) 'displeasing alike to God
and to the enemies of God,' when he comes
boldly to the throne of grace, not to find
grace and mercy, because he feels that he
needs them: but to boast of God's grace,
and make God's mercy to him an excuse
for looking down upon his fellow-creatures;
and worships, like the Pharisee, in self-conceit
and pride, thanking God that he is not as
other men are?

Better far to be the publican, who stood
afar off, and dare not lift up as much as his
eyes toward heaven, but cried only, 'God be
merciful to me a sinner.' Better far to be the
honest and devout soldier, who, when Jesus

offered to come to his house, answered, 'Lord, I am not worthy that thou shouldest 'enter under my roof. But speak the word 'only, and my servant shall be healed.'

Only he must say that in honesty, in spirit, and in truth, like St. Peter. For a man may shrink from religion, from the thought of God, from coming to the Holy Communion, for two most opposite reasons.

He may shrink from them because he knows he is full of sins, and wishes to keep his sins; and knows that, if he worships God, if he comes to the Holy Communion—indeed, if he remembers the presence of God at all, —he pledges himself to give up his bad habits; to repent and amend, which is just what he has no mind to do. So he turns away from God, because he chooses to remain bad. May the Lord have mercy on his soul, for he has no mercy on it himself! He chooses evil, and refuses good; and evil will be his ruin.

But, again, a man may shrink from God, from church, from the Holy Communion, because he feels himself bad, and longs to be good; because he feels himself full of evil habits, and hates them, and sees how ugly they are, and is afraid to appear in the presence of God foul with sin.

Let him be of good cheer. He is not going wrong wilfully. But he is making a mistake. Let him make it no more. He feels himself unworthy. Let him come all the more, that he may be made worthy. Let him come, because he is worthy. For—strange it may seem, but true it is—that a man is the more worthy to draw near to God the more he feels himself to be utterly unworthy thereof.

He who partakes worthily of the Holy Communion is he who says with his whole heart, 'We are not worthy so much as to gather up the crumbs under thy table.' He with whom Christ will take up his abode is he who says, 'Lord, I am not worthy that thou shouldest enter under my roof.'

For humility is the beginning of all goodness, and the end of all wisdom.

'He who says that he sees is blind. He who knows his own blindness sees. He who says he has no sin in him is the sinner. He who confesses his sins is the righteous man; for God is faithful and just to forgive him, as he did St. Peter, and to cleanse him from all unrighteousness.

SERMON XIX.

A WHITSUN SERMON.

Psalm civ. 24, 27—30.

O Lord, how manifold are thy works! in wisdom hast thou made them all: the earth is full of thy riches. . . . These wait all upon thee; that thou mayest give them their meat in due season. That thou givest them they gather: thou openest thine hand, they are filled with good. Thou hidest thy face, they are troubled: thou takest away their breath, they die, and return to their dust. Thou sendest forth thy Spirit, they are created: and thou renewest the face of the earth.

YOU may not understand why I read this morning, instead of the *Te Deum*, the 'Song of the three Children,' which calls on all powers and creatures in the world to bless and praise God. You may not understand also, at first, why this grand 104th Psalm was chosen as one of the special Psalms for

Whitsuntide,—what it has to do with the Holy Ghost, the Comforter, the Spirit of God. Let me try to explain it to you, and may God grant that you may find something worth remembering among my clumsy words.

You were told this morning that there were two ways of learning concerning God and the Spirit of God,—that one was by the hearing of the ear, and the Holy Bible; the other by the seeing of the eye—by nature and the world around us. It is of the latter I speak this afternoon,—of what you can learn concerning God by seeing, if only you have eyes, and the same Spirit of God to open those eyes, as the Psalmist had.

The man who wrote this Psalm looked round him on the wondrous world in which we dwell, and all he saw in it spoke to him of God; of one God, boundless in wisdom and in power, in love and care; and of one Spirit of God, the Lord and Giver of Life.

He saw all this, and so glorious did it seem to him, as he looked on the fair world round him, that he could not contain himself. Not only was his reason satisfied, but his heart was touched. It was so glorious that he could not speak of it coldly, calmly; and he burst out into singing a song of praise—'O 'Lord our God, thou art become exceeding 'glorious; thou art clothed with majesty and 'honour.' For he saw everywhere order; all things working together for good. He saw everywhere order and rule; and something within him told him, there must be a Lawgiver, an Orderer, a Ruler, and he must be One.

Again, the Psalmist saw everywhere a purpose; things evidently created to be of use to each other. And the Spirit of God told him there must be One who purposed all this; who meant to do it, and who had done it; who thought it out and planned it by wisdom and understanding.

Then the Psalmist saw how everything, from the highest to the lowest, was of use. The fir trees were a dwelling for the stork; and the very stony rocks, where nothing else can live, were a refuge for the wild goats; everywhere he saw use and bounty—food, shelter, life, happiness, given to man and beast, and not earned by them; then he said—'There must be a bountiful Lord, a 'Giver, generous and loving, from whom the 'very lions seek their meat, when they roar 'after their prey; on whom all the creeping 'things innumerable wait in the great sea, 'that he may give them meat in due 'season.'

But, moreover, he saw everywhere beauty; shapes, and colours, and sounds, which were beautiful in his eyes, and gave him pleasure deep and strange, he knew not why: and the Spirit of God within him told him—'These 'fair things please thee. Do they not please 'Him who made them? He that formed the 'ear, shall he not hear the song of birds? 'He that made the eye, shall he not see the 'colours of the flowers? He who made thee 'to rejoice in the beauty of the earth, shall 'not he rejoice in his own works?' And God seemed to him, in his mind's eye, to delight in his own works, as a painter delights in the picture which he has drawn, as a gardener delights in the flowers which he has planted;

as a cunning workman delights in the curious machine which he has invented; as a king delights in the fair parks and gardens and stately palaces which he has laid out, and builded, and adorned, for his own pleasure, as well as for the good of his subjects.

And then, beneath all, and beyond all, there came to him another question—What is life?

The painter paints his picture, but it has no life. The workman makes his machine, but, though it moves and works, it has no life. The gardener,—his flowers have life, but he has not given it to them; he can only sow the seemingly dead seeds. Who is He that giveth those seeds a body as it pleases him, and to every seed its own body, its own growth of leaf, form, and colour? God alone. And what is that life which he does give? Who can tell that? What is life? What is it which changes the seed into a flower, the egg into a bird? It is not the seed itself; the egg itself. What power or will have they, over themselves? It is not in the seed, or in the egg, as all now know from experience. You may look for it with all the microscopes in the world, but you will not find it. There is nothing to be found by the eyes of mortal man which can account for the growth and life of any created thing.

And what is death? What does the live thing lose, when it loses life? This moment the bird was alive; a tiny pellet of shot has gone through its brain, and now its life is lost: but what is lost? It is just the same size, shape, colour; it weighs exactly the same as it did when alive. What is the thing not to be seen, touched, weighed, described, or understood, which it has lost, which we call life?

And to that deep question the Psalmist had an answer whispered to him,—a hint only, as it were, in a parable. Life is the breath of God. It is the Spirit of God, who is the Lord and Giver of life. God breathes into things the breath of life. When he takes away that breath they die, and are turned again to their dust. When he lets his breath go forth again, they are made, and he renews the face of the earth.

That is enough for thee, O man, to know. What life is thou canst not know. Thou canst only speak of it in a figure—as the breath, the Spirit of God. That Spirit of God is not the universe itself. But he is working in all things, giving them form and life, dividing to each severally as he will; all their shape, their beauty, their powers, their instincts, their thoughts; all in them save brute matter and dead dust: from him they come, and to him they return again. All order, all law, all force, all usefulness, come from him. He is the Lord and Giver of life, in whom all things live, and move, and have their being.

Therefore, my friends, let us at all times, in all places, and especially at this Whitsuntide, remember that all we see, or can see, except sin, is the work of the Holy Ghost, the Spirit of God. Let us look on the world around us, as what it is, as what the old Psalmist saw it to be,—a sacred place, full of God's presence, shaped, quickened, and guided by the Spirit of God, the Lord and Giver of life.

My dear friends, God grant that you may

all learn to look upon this world as the Psalmist looked on it. God grant that you may all learn to see, each in your own way, what a great and pious poet of our fathers' time put into words far wiser and grander than any which I can invent for you, when he said how, looking on the earth, the sea, the sky, he felt—

> ' A presence that disturbs me with the joy
> Of elevated thoughts; a sense sublime
> Of something far more deeply interfused,
> Whose dwelling is the light of setting suns,
> And the round ocean, and the living air,
> And the blue sky, and in the mind of man :
> A motion and a spirit that impels
> All thinking things, all objects of all thought,
> And rolls through all things. Therefore am I still
> A lover of the meadows and the woods
> And mountains ; and of all that we behold
> From this green earth ; of all the mighty world ;
> Of eye and ear, both what they half create
> And what perceive ; well pleased to recognise
> In nature and the language of the sense
> The anchor of my purest thoughts, the nurse,
> The guide, the guardian of my heart, and soul
> Of all my moral being.' *

---

* Wordsworth's 'Ode on Tintern Abbey.'

'Of all my moral being.'

Yes; of our moral being, our characters, our souls. By looking upon this beautiful and wonderful world around us with reverence, and earnestness, and love, as what it is,—the work of God's Spirit,—we shall become not merely the more learned, or the more happy, we shall become actually better men. The beauties in the earth and sky; the flowers with their fair hues and fragrant scents; the song of birds; the green shaughs and woodlands; the moors purple with heath, and golden with furze; the shapes of clouds, from the delicate mist upon the lawn to the thunder pillar towering up in awful might; the sunrise and sunset, painted by God afresh each morn and even; the blue sky, which is the image of God the heavenly Father, boundless, clear, and calm, looking down on all below with the same smile of love, sending his rain alike on the evil and on the good, and causing his sun to shine alike on the just and on the unjust:—he who watches all these things, day by day, will find his heart grow quiet, sober, meek, contented. His eyes will be turned away from beholding vanity. His soul will be kept from vexation of spirit. In God's tabernacle, which is the universe of all the worlds, he will be kept from the strife of tongues. As he watches the work of God's Spirit, the beauty of God's Spirit, the wisdom of God's Spirit, the fruitfulness of God's Spirit, which shines forth in every wayside flower, and every gnat which dances in the sun, he will rejoice in God's work, even as God himself rejoices. He will learn to value things at their true price, and see things of their real size. Ambition, fame, money, will seem small things to him as he considers the lilies of the field, how the heavenly Father clothes them, and the birds of the air, how the heavenly Father feeds them; and he will say with the wise man—

> 'All the windy ways of men
> Are but dust that rises up,
> And is lightly laid again.'

Dust, indeed, and not worthy the attention of the wise man, who considers how the very heaven and earth shall perish, and yet God endure; how—'They all shall wax old as

'doth a garment, and as a vesture shall God
'change them, and they shall be changed:
'but God is the same, and his years shall
'not fail.'

And as that man grows more quiet, he will grow more loving likewise; more merciful to the very dumb animals. He will be ashamed even to disturb a bird upon its nest, when he remembers the builder and maker of that nest is not the bird alone, but God. He will believe the words of the wise man—

> 'He prayeth well who loveth well
>   Both man, and bird, and beast.
> He prayeth best who loveth best
>   All things, both great and small;
> For the great God who loveth us,
>   He made and loveth all.'

More quiet, more loving will that man grow; and more pious likewise. For there ought to come to that man a sense of God's presence, of God's nearness, which will fill him with a wholesome fear of God. As he sees with the inward eyes of his reason God's Spirit at work for ever on every seed, on every insect, ay, on every nerve and muscle of his own body, he will heartily say with the Psalmist—'I will give thanks unto thee, 'for I am fearfully and wonderfully made. 'Marvellous are thy works, and that my soul 'knoweth right well. Thine eyes did see my 'substance, yet being imperfect; and in thy 'book were all my members written, which 'day by day were fashioned, when as yet 'there was none of them. Whither shall I 'go then from thy Spirit, or whither shall I 'flee from thy presence? If I climb up to 'heaven, thou art there; if I go down to 'hell, thou art there also; if I take the wings 'of the morning, and dwell in the uttermost 'parts of the sea, even there thy hand shall 'lead me, and thy right hand hold me still. 'If I say, Peradventure the darkness shall 'cover me, then shall my night be turned 'into day.'

Yes, God he will see is everywhere, over all, and through all, and in all; and from God there is no escape. The only hope, the only wisdom, is to open his heart to God as a child to its father, and cry with the Psalmist

—'Try me, O God, and search the ground 'of my heart; prove me, and examine my 'thoughts. Look well if there be any way 'of wickedness in me, and lead me in the 'way everlasting.'

My dear friends, take these thoughts home with you: and may God give you grace to ponder over them, and so make your Whitsun holiday more quiet, more pure, more full of lessons learnt from God's great green book which lies outside for every man to read. Of such as you said the wise heathen long ago—'Too happy are they who till the land, if they but knew the blessings which they have.'

And it is a blessing, a privilege, and therefore a responsibility laid on you by your Father and your Saviour, to have such a fair, peaceful, country scene around you, as you will behold when you leave this church, —a scene where everything is to the wise man, where everything should be to you, a witness of God's Spirit; a witness of God's power, God's wisdom, God's care, God's love. Go, and may God turn away your hearts from all that is mean and selfish, all that is coarse and low, and lift them up unto himself, as you look upon the fields, and woods, and sky, till you, too, say with the Psalmist —' O Lord, how manifold are thy works! in 'wisdom hast thou made them all: the earth 'is full of thy riches. I will praise my God 'while I have my being; my joy shall be in 'the Lord.'

SERMON XX.

SELF-HELP.

St. John xvi. 7.

It is expedient for you that I go away : for if I go not away, the Comforter will not come unto you; but if I depart, I will send him unto you.

THIS is a deep and strange saying. How can it be expedient, useful, or profitable, for any human being that Christ should go away from them? To be in Christ's presence; to see his face; to hear his voice;—would not this be the most expedient and profitable, yea, the most blessed and blissful of things which could befall us? Is it not that which saints hope to attain for ever in heaven—the beatific vision of Christ?

My dear friends, one thing is certain, that Christ loves us far better than we can love ourselves, and knows how to show that love.

He would have stayed with the apostles, instead of ascending into heaven, if it had been expedient for them. Yea, if it had been expedient for him to have stayed on earth among mankind unto this very day, he would have stayed.

Because it was not expedient, not good for the apostles, not good for mankind, that he should stay among them, therefore he ascended into heaven, and sat down at the right hand of God, all authority and power being given to him in heaven and in earth.

And he gives us a reason for so doing—only a hint; but still a hint, by which we may see to-day it was expedient for us that he should go away.

Unless he went away, the Comforter would not come. Now the true and exact meaning of the Comforter is the Strengthener, the Encourager—one who gives a man strength of mind, and courage of spirit, to do his work. Without that Comforter, the apostles would be weak and spiritless. Without being encouraged and inspired by him, they would never get through the work which they had to do, of preaching the Gospel to the whole world.

We may surely see, if we think, some of the cause of this. The apostles, till our Lord's ascension, had been following him about like scholars following a master—almost like children holding by their father's hand. They had had no will of their own; no opinion of their own; they had never had to judge for themselves, or act for themselves; and, when they had tried to do so, they had always been in the wrong, and Christ had rebuked them. They had been like scholars, I say, with a teacher, or children with a parent. Yea rather, when one remembers who they were, poor fishermen, and who he was—God made man—they had been (I speak with all reverence) as dogs at their master's side—faithful and intelligent truly; but with no will of their own, looking for ever up to his hand and his eye, to see what he would have them do. But that could not last. It ought not to last. God does not wish us to be always as animals, not even always as children; he wishes us to become men; perfect men, who have their senses exercised by experience to discern good and evil.

And so it was to be with the apostles. They had to learn, as we all have to learn, self-help, self-government, self-determination. They were to think for themselves, and act for themselves; and yet not by themselves. For he would put into them a spirit, even his Spirit; and so, when they were thinking for themselves, they would be thinking as he would have them think; when they were acting for themselves, they would be acting as he would have them act. They would live; but not their own life, for Christ would live in them. They would speak: but not their own words; the Spirit of their Father would speak in them; that so they might come in the unity of the faith, and the knowledge of the Son of God, to be perfect men, to the measure of the stature of the fulness of Christ.

My dear friends, this may seem deep and a mystery: but so are all things in this wondrous life of ours. And surely we see a pattern of all this in our own lives. Each child is educated—or ought to be—as Christ educated his apostles.

Have we not had, some of us, in early life some parent, friend, teacher, spiritual pastor, or master, to whom we looked up with unbounded respect? His word to us was law. His counsel was as the oracles of God. We did not dream of thinking for ourselves, acting for ourselves, while we had him to tell us how to think, how to act; and we were happy in our devotion. We felt what a blessed thing, not merely protecting and guiding, but elevating and ennobling, was reverence and obedience to one wiser and better than ourselves. But that did not last. It could not last. Our teacher was taken from us; perhaps by mere change of place, and the chances of this mortal life; perhaps by death, which sunders all fair bonds upon this side the grave. Perhaps, most painful of all, we began to differ from our teacher; to find that, though we respected and loved him still, though we felt a deep debt of thanks to him for what he had taught us, we could not quite agree in all; we had begun to think for ourselves, and we found that we must think for ourselves; and the new responsibility was very heavy. We felt like young birds thrust out of the nest to shift for themselves in the wide world.

But, after a while, we found that we could think, could act for ourselves, as we never expected to do. We found that we were no more children: that we were improving in manly virtues by having to bear our own burdens; and to acquire,

'The reason firm, the temperate will,
Endurance, foresight, strength, and skill.

And we found, too, that though our old teachers were parted from us, yet they were with us still; that (to compare small things with great, and Christ's servants with their Lord) a spirit came to us from them, and brought all things to our remembrance, whatsoever they had said to us; that we remembered their words more vividly, we understood their meaning more fully and deeply, now that they were parted, than we did when they were with us. We loved them as well, ay, better, than of old, for we saw more clearly what a debt we owed to them; and so it was, after all, expedient for us that they should have gone away. That parting with them, which seemed so dangerous to us, as well as painful, really comforted us—strengthened and encouraged us to become stronger and braver souls, full of self-help, self-government, self-determination.

And so we shall find it, I believe, in our religion.

We may say with a sigh, 'Ah, that I 'could see my Lord and Saviour. I should ' be safe then. I dare not sin then.'

It may be so. I am the last to deny that our Lord Jesus Christ has (as he certainly could, if he chose) shown himself bodily to certain of his saints (as he showed himself to St. Paul and to St. Stephen) in order to strengthen their faith in some great trial. But if it had been good for us in general to see the Lord in this life, doubt not that we should have seen him. And because we do not see him, be sure that it is not good.

We may say, again, 'Ah that the Lord 'Jesus had but remained on earth, what just 'laws, what peace and prosperity would the 'world have enjoyed! Wars would have 'ceased long ago; oppression and injustice 'would be unknown.'

It may be so. And yet again it may not. Perhaps our Lord's staying on earth would have had some quite different effect, of which we cannot even dream; and done, not good, but harm. Let us have faith in him. Let us believe in his perfect wisdom, and in his perfect love. Let us believe that he is educating us, as he educated the apostles, by going away. That he is by his absence helping men to help themselves, teaching men to teach themselves, guiding and governing men to guide and govern themselves by that law of liberty which is the law of his Spirit; to love the right, and to do the right, not from fear of punishment, but of their own heart and will.

For remember, he has not left us comfortless. He has not merely given us commands; he has given us the power of understanding, valuing, obeying these commands. For his Spirit is with us; the Spirit of Whitsuntide; the Comforter, the Encourager, the Strengthener, by whom we may both perceive and know what we ought to do, and also have grace and power faithfully to fulfil the same.

Come to yonder holy table this day, and there claim your share in Christ, who is absent from you in the body, but ever present in the spirit. Come to that table, that you may live by Christ's life, and learn to love what he commandeth, and desire what he doth promise, that so your hearts may surely there be fixed, where true joys are to be found; namely, in the gracious motions and heavenly inspirations of the Holy Ghost the Comforter, who proceedeth from the Father and the Son.

SERMON XXI.

ENDURANCE.

1 PETER II. 19.

This is thankworthy, if a man for conscience toward God endure grief, suffering wrongfully.

THIS is a great epistle, this epistle for the day, and full of deep lessons. Let us try to learn some of them.

'What glory is it,' St. Peter says, 'if, when 'ye be beaten for your faults, ye take it 'patiently?' What credit is it to a man, if, having broken the law, he submits to be punished? The man who will not do that, the man who resists punishment, is not a civilized man, but a savage and a mere animal. If he will not live under discipline, if he expects to break the law with impunity, he makes himself an outlaw; he puts himself by his rebellion outside the law, and becomes unfit for society, a public enemy of his fellow-men. The first lesson which men have to learn, which even the heathen have learnt, as soon as they have risen above mere savages, is the sacredness of law—the necessity of punishment for those who break the law.

The Jews had this feeling of the sacredness of law. Moses' divine law had taught it them. The Romans, heathen though they were, had the same feeling—that law was sacred; that men must obey law. And the good thing which they did for the world (though they did it at the expense of bloodshed and cruelty without end) was the bringing all the lawless nations and wild tribes about them under strict law, and drilling them into order and obedience. That it was, which gave the Roman power strength and success for many centuries.

But above the kingdom of law, which says to a man merely, 'Thou shalt not do wrong: and if thou dost, thou shalt be punished,' there is another kingdom, far deeper, wider, nobler; even the kingdom of grace, which

says to a man, not merely, 'Do not do wrong,' but 'Do right;' and not only 'Do right for fear of being punished,' but 'Do
' right because it is right; do right because
' thou hast grace in thy heart; even the grace
' of God, and the Spirit of God, which makes
' thee love what is right, and see how right it
' is, and how beautiful; so that thou must fol-
' low after the right, not from fear of punish-
' ment, but in spite of fear of punishment;
' follow after the right, not when it is safe
' only, but when it is dangerous; not when it
' is honourable only in the eyes of men, but
' when it is despised. If thou hast God's
' grace in thy heart; if thou lovest what is
' right with the true love, which is the Spirit of
' God, then thou wilt never stop to ask, "Will
' it pay me to do right?" Thou wilt feel that
' the right thou must do, whether it pays thee
' or not; still loving the right, and cleaving
' steadfastly to the right, through disappoint-
' ment, poverty, shame, trouble, death itself,
' if need be: if only thou canst keep a conscience void of offence toward God and
' man.'

'But shall I have no reward?' asks a man, 'for doing right? Am I to give up a hundred pleasant things for conscience' sake, 'and get nothing in return?' Yes: there is a reward for righteousness, even in this life. God repays those who make sacrifices for conscience' sake, I verily believe, in most cases, a hundred fold in this life. In this life it stands true, that he who loses his life shall save it; that he who goes through the world with a single eye to duty, without selfishness, without vanity, without ambition, careless whether he be laughed at, careless whether he be ill-used, provided only his conscience acquits him, and God's approving smile is on him—in this life it stands true that that man is the happiest man after all; that that man is the most prosperous man after all; that, like Christ, when he was doing his Father's work, he has meat to eat and strengthen him in his life's journey, which the world knows not of. But if not; if it seem good to God to let him taste the bitters, and not the sweets, of doing right, in this life; if it seem good to God that he should suffer—as many a man and woman too has suffered for doing right—nothing but contempt, neglect, prison, and death; is he worse off than Jesus Christ, his Lord, was before him? Shall the disciple be above his master? What if he have to drink of the cup of sorrow of which Christ drank, and be baptized with the baptism of martyrdom with which Christ was baptized? Where is he, but where the Son of God has been already? What is he doing, but treading in the steps of Christ crucified; that he may share in the blessing and glory and honour without end which God the Father heaped upon Christ his Son, because he was perfect in duty, perfect in love of right, perfect in resignation, perfect in submission under injustice, perfect in forgiveness of his murderers, perfect in faith in the justice and mercy of God: who did no sin—that is, never injured his own cause by anger or revenge; and had no guile in his mouth—that is, never prevaricated, lied, concealed his opinions, for fear of the consequences, however terrible; but before the chief priests and Pontius Pilate witnessed a good confession, though he knew that it would bring on him a dreadful death; who, when he was reviled, reviled not again, but committed himself to him who judgeth righteously—the meekest of all beings, and in that very meekness the strongest of all beings; the most utterly resigned, and by that very resignation the most heroic—the being who seemed, on the cross of Calvary, most utterly conquered by injustice and violence: but who, by that very cross, conquered the whole world.

This is a great mystery, and hard to learn. Flesh and blood, our animal nature, will never compass it all; for it belongs, not to the flesh, but to the spirit. But our spirits, our immortal souls, may learn the lesson at last, if we feed them continually with the thought of Christ; if we meditate upon whatsoever things are true, whatsoever things are honourable, just, pure, lovely, and of good report. Then we may learn, at last, after many failures, and many sorrows of heart, that the spirit is stronger than the flesh; that meekness is stronger than wrath, silence stronger than shouting, peace stronger than war, forgiveness stronger than vengeance, just as Christ hanging on his cross was stronger—exercising a more vast and miraculous effect on the hearts of men—than if he had called whole armies of angels to destroy his enemies, like one of the old kings and conquerors of the earth, whose works have perished with themselves.

Yes, gradually we must learn that our strength is to sit still; that to do well and suffer for it, instead of returning evil for evil, and railing for railing, is to show forth the spirit of Christ, and to enter into the joy of our Lord.

The statesman debating in Parliament; the conqueror changing the fate of nations on bloody battle-fields; these all do their work; and are needful, doubtless, in a sinful, piecemeal world like this. But there are those of whom the noisy world never hears, who have chosen the better part which shall not be taken from them; who enter into a higher glory than that of statesmen, or conquerors, or the successful and famous of the earth. Many a man—clergyman or layman—struggling in poverty and obscurity, with daily toil of body and mind, to make his fellow-creatures better and happier; many a poor woman, bearing children in pain and sorrow, and bringing them up with pain and sorrow, but in industry, too, and piety; or submitting without complaint to a brutal husband; or sacrificing all her own hopes in life to feed and educate her brothers and sisters; or enduring for years the peevishness and troublesomeness of some relation;—all these (and the world which God sees is full of such, though the world which man sees takes no note of them)—gentle souls, humble souls, uncomplaining souls, suffering souls, pious souls—these are God's elect; these are Christ's sheep; these are the salt of the earth, who, by doing each their little duty as unto God, not unto men, keep society from decaying more than do all the constitutions and acts of parliament which statesmen ever invented. These are they—though they little dream of any such honour—who copy the likeness of the old martyrs, who did well and suffered for it; and the likeness of Christ, of whom it was said, 'He shall not

'strive nor cry, neither shall his voice be
'heard in the streets.'

For what was it in the old martyrs which made men look up to them, as persons infinitely better than themselves, with quite unmeasurable admiration; so that they worshipped them after their deaths, as if they had been gods rather than men?

It was this. The world in old times had been admiring successful people, just as it does at this day. Was a man powerful, rich? Had he slaves by the hundred? Was his table loaded with the richest meats and wines? Could he indulge every pleasure and fancy of his own? Could he heap his friends with benefits? Could he ruin or destroy any one who thwarted him? In one word, was he a mighty and successful tyrant? Then that was the man to honour and worship; that was the sort of man to become, if anyone had the chance, by fair means or foul. Just as the world worships now the successful man; and—if you will but make a million of money—will flatter you and court you, and never ask either how you made your money, or how you spend your money; or whether you are a good man or a bad one: for money in man's eyes, as charity in God's eyes, covereth a multitude of sins; and as long as thou doest well unto thyself, men will speak well of thee.

But there arose, in that wicked old world in which St. Paul lived, an entirely new sort of people—people who did not wish to be successful; did not wish to be rich; did not wish to be powerful; did not wish for pleasures and luxuries which this world could give: who only wished to be good; to do right, and to teach others to do right. Christians, they were called; after Christ their Lord and God. Weak old men, poor women, slaves, even children, were among them. Not many mighty, not many rich, not many noble, were called. They were mostly weak and oppressed people, who had been taught by suffering and sorrow.

One would have thought that the world would have despised these Christians, and let them go their own way in peace. But it was not so. The mighty of this world, and those who lived by pandering to their vices, so far from despising the Christians, saw at once how important they were. They saw that, if people went about the world determined to speak nothing but what they believed to be true, and to do nothing but what was right, then the wicked world would be indeed turned upside down, and, as they complained against St. Paul more than once, the hope of their gains would be gone. Therefore they conceived the most bitter hatred against these Christians, and rose against them, for the same simple reason that Cain rose up against Abel and slew him, because his works were wicked, and his brother's righteous. They argued with them; they threatened them; they tried to terrify them: but they found to their astonishment that the Christians would not change their minds for any terror. Then their hatred became rage and fury. They could not understand how such poor ignorant contemptible people as the Christians seemed to be, dared to have an opinion of their own, and to stand to it; how they dared to think themselves right, and all the world wrong; and in their fury they inflicted on them tortures to read of which should make the blood run cold. And their rage and fury increased to madness, when they found that these Christians, instead of complaining, instead of rebelling, instead of trying to avenge themselves, submitted to all their sufferings, not only patiently and uncomplaining, but joyfully, and as an honour and a glory. Some, no doubt, they conquered by torture, agony, and terror; and so made them deny Christ, and return to the wickedness of the heathen. But those renegades were always miserable. Their own consciences condemned them. They felt they had sold their own souls for a lie; and many of them, in their agony of mind, repented again, like St. Peter after he had denied his Lord through fear, proclaimed themselves Christians after all, went through all their tortures a second time, and died triumphant over death and hell.

But there were those—to be counted by hundreds, if not thousands—who dared all, and endured all; and won (as it was rightly called) the crown of martyrdom. Feeble old men, weak women, poor slaves, even little children, sealed their testimony with their blood, and conquered, not by fighting, but by suffering.

They conquered. They conquered for themselves in the next world; for they went to heaven and bliss, and their light affliction, which was but for a moment, worked out for them an exceeding and eternal weight of glory.

They conquered in this world also. For the very world which had scourged them, racked them, crucified them, burned them alive, when they were dead turned round and worshipped them as heroes, almost as divine beings. And they were divine; for they had in them the Divine Spirit, the Spirit of God and of Christ. Therefore the foolish world was awed, conscience-stricken, pricked to the heart, when it looked on those whom it had pierced, as it had pierced Christ the Lord, and cried, as the centurion cried on Calvary, 'Surely these were the sons and ' daughters of God. Surely there was some-

'thing more divine, more noble, more beau-
'tiful in these poor creatures dying in torture,
'than in all the tyrants and conquerors and
'rich men of the earth. This is the true
'greatness, this is the true heroism—to do
'well and suffer for it patiently.'

And thenceforth men began to get, slowly but surely, a quite new idea of true greatness; they learnt to see that not revenge, but forgiveness; not violence, but resignation; not success, but holiness, are the perfection of humanity. They began to have a reverence for those who were weak in body, and simple in heart,—a reverence for women, for children, for slaves, for all whom the world despises, such as the old Egyptians, Greeks, Romans, had never had. They began to see that God could make strong the weak things of this world, and glorify himself in the courage and honesty of the poorest and the meanest. They began to see that in Christ Jesus was neither male nor female, Jew nor Greek, barbarian, Scythian, slave or free, but that all were one in Christ Jesus, all alike capable of receiving the Spirit of God, all alike children of the one Father, who was above all, and in all, and with them all.

And so the endurance and the sufferings of the early martyrs was the triumph of good over evil; the triumph of honesty and truth; of purity and virtue; of gentleness and patience; of faith in a just and loving God: because it was the triumph of the Spirit of Christ, by which he died, and rose again, and conquered shame and pain, and death and hell.

SERMON XXII.

TOLERATION.

(Preached at Christ Church, Marylebone, 1867, for the Bishop of London's Fund.)

MATTHEW XIII. 24—30.

The kingdom of heaven is likened unto a man which sowed good seed in his field: but while men slept, his enemy came and sowed tares among the wheat, and went his way. But when the blade was sprung up, and brought forth fruit, then appeared the tares also. So the servants of the household came and said unto him, Sir, didst not thou sow good seed in thy field? from whence then hath it tares? He said unto them, An enemy hath done this. The servants said unto him, Wilt thou then that we go and gather them up? But he said, Nay; lest while ye gather up the tares, ye root up also the wheat with them. Let both grow together until the harvest: and in the time of harvest I will say to the reapers, Gather ye together first the tares, and bind them in bundles to burn them: but gather the wheat into my barn.

THE thoughtful man who wishes well to the Gospel of Christ will hardly hear this parable without a feeling of humiliation.

None of our Lord's parables are more clear and simple in their meaning; none have a more direct and practical command appended to them; none have been less regarded during the last fifteen hundred years. <u>Toleration, solemnly enjoined, has been the exception.</u> <u>Persecution, solemnly forbidden, has been the rule.</u> Men, as usual, have fancied themselves wiser than God; for they have believed themselves wise enough to do what he had told them that they were not wise enough to do, and so have tried to root the tares from among the wheat. Men have, as usual, <u>lacked faith in Christ</u>; they did not believe that he was actually governing the earth which belonged to him; that he was actually cultivating his field, the world: they therefore believed themselves bound to do for him what he neglected, or at least did not see fit, to do for himself; and they tried to root up the tares from among the wheat. They have tried to repress free thought, and to silence novel opinions, forgetful that Christ must have been right after all, and that in silencing opinions which startled them, they might be quenching the Spirit, and despising prophecies. But they found it more difficult to quench the Spirit than they fancied, when they began the policy of repression. They have found that the Spirit blew where it listed, and they heard the sound of it, but knew not whence it came, or whither it went; that the utterances which startled them, the tones of feeling and thought which terrified them, reappeared, though crushed in one place, suddenly in another; that the whole atmosphere was charged with them, as with electricity; and that it was impossible to say where the unseen force might not concentrate itself at any moment, and flash out in a lightning stroke. Then their fear has turned to a rage. They have thought no more of putting down opinions: but of putting down men. They have found it more difficult than they fancied to separate the man from his opinions; to hate the sin and love the sinner: and so they have begun to persecute; and, finding brute force, or at least the chichane of law, far more easy than either convincing their opponents or allowing themselves to be convinced by them, they have fined, imprisoned, tortured, burnt, exterminated; and, like the Roman conquerors of old, 'made a desert, and called that peace.'

And all the while the words stood written in the Scriptures which they professed to believe: 'Nay: lest while ye root up the tares, ye root up the wheat also.'

They had been told, if ever men were told, that the work was beyond their powers of discernment: that, whatever the tares were, or however they came into God's field the world, they were either too like the wheat, or too intimately entangled with them, for any mortal man to part them. God would part them in his own good time. If they trusted God, they would let them be; certain that he hated what was false, what was hurtful, infinitely more than they; certain that he would some day cast out of his kingdom all things which offend, and all that work injustice, and whatsoever loveth and maketh a lie; and that, therefore, if he suffered such things to abide awhile, it was for them to submit, and to believe that God loved the world better than they, and knew better how to govern it. But if, on the contrary, they did not believe God, then they would set to work, in their disobedient self-conceit, to do that which he had forbidden them; and the certain result would be that, with the tares, they would root up the wheat likewise.

Note here two things. First, it is not said that there were no tares among the wheat; nor that the servants would fail in rooting some of them up. They would succeed probably in doing some good: but they would succeed certainly in doing more harm. In their short-sighted, blind, erring, hasty zeal, they would destroy the good with the evil. Their knowledge of this complex and miraculous universe was too shallow, their canons of criticism were too narrow, to decide on what ought, or ought not, to grow in the field of him whose ways and thoughts were as much higher than theirs as the heaven is higher than the earth.

Note also, that the Lord does not blame

them for their purpose. He merely points out to them its danger; and forbids it because it is dangerous; for their wish to root out the tares was not 'natural.' We shall libel it by calling it that. It was distinctly spiritual, the first impulse of spiritual men, who love right, and hate wrong, and desire to cultivate the one, and exterminate the other. To root out the tares; to put down bad men and wrong thoughts by force, is one of the earliest religious instincts. It is the child's instinct—pardonable though mistaken. The natural man—whether the heathen savage at one end of the scale, or the epicurean man of the world at the other—has no such instinct. He will feel no anger against falsehood, because he has no love for truth; he will be liberal enough, tolerant enough, of all which does not touch his own self-interest; but that once threatened, he too may join the ranks of the bigots, and persecute, not like them, in the name of God and truth, but in those of society and order; and so the chief priests and Pontius Pilate may make common cause. And yet the chief priests, with their sense of duty, of truth, and of right, however blundering, concealed, perverted, may be a whole moral heaven higher than Pilate with no sense of aught beyond present expediency. But nevertheless what have been the consequences to both? That the chief priests have failed as utterly as the Pilates. As God forewarned them, they have rooted up the wheat with the tares; they have made the blood of martyrs the seed of the Church; and more, they have made martyrs of those who never deserved to be martyrs, by wholesale and indiscriminate condemnation. They have forgotten that the wheat and the tares grow together, not merely in separate men, but in each man's own heart and thoughts; that light and darkness, wisdom and folly, duty and ambition, self-sacrifice and self-conceit, are fighting in every soul of man in whom there is even the germ of spiritual life. Therefore they have made men offenders for a word. They have despised noble aspirations, ignored deep and sound insights, because they came in questionable shapes, mingled with errors or eccentricities. They have cried in their haste, 'Here are tares, and tares alone.'

Again and again have religious men done this, for many a hundred years; and again and again the Nemesis has fallen on them. A generation or two has passed, and the world has revolted from their unjust judgments. It has perceived, among the evil, good which it had overlooked in an indignant haste and passionateness, learnt from those who should have taught it wisdom, patience, and charity. It has made heroes of those who had been branded as heretics; and has cried, 'There was wheat, and wheat alone;' and so religious men have hindered the very cause for which they fancied that they were fighting; and have gained nothing by disobeying God's command, save to weaken their own moral influence, to increase the divisions of the Church, and to put a fresh stumbling-block in the path of the ignorant and the young.

And what have been the consequences to Christ's Church? Have not her enemies—

and her friends too—for centuries past, cried in vain:—

> 'For forms of faith let graceless zealots fight,
> His can't be wrong, whose life is in the right.'

Of Christian morals her enemies have not complained: but that these morals have been postponed, neglected, forgotten, in the disputes over abstruse doctrines, over ceremonies, and over no-ceremonies; that men who were all fully agreed in their definition of goodness, and what a good man should be and do, have denounced each other concerning matters which had no influence whatsoever to practical morality, till the ungodly cried, 'See how these Christians 'hate one another! See how they waste 'their time in disputing concerning the acci-'dents of the bread of life, forgetful that thousands were perishing round them for want of any bread of life at all!'

My friends, these things are true; and have been true for centuries. Let us not try to forget them by denouncing them as the utterances of the malevolent and the unbelieving. Let us rather imitate the wise man who said, that he was always grateful to his critics, for, however unjust their attacks, they were certain to attack, and therefore to show him, his weakest points. And here is our weakest point; namely, in our unhappy divisions—which are the fruits of selfwill and self-conceit, and of the vain attempt to do that which God incarnate has told us we cannot do—to part the wheat from the tares.

We cannot part them. Man could never do it, even in the simpler Middle Age. Far less can he do it now in an age full of such strange, such complex influences; at once so progressive and conservative; an age in which the same man is often craving after some new prospect of the future, and craving at the same moment after the seemingly obsolete past; longing for fresh truth, and yet dreading to lose the old; with hope struggling against fear, courage against modesty, scorn of imbecility against reverence for authority in the same man's heart, while the mystery of the new world around him strives with the mystery of the old world which lies behind him; while the belief that man is the same being now as he was five thousand years ago strives with the plain fact that he is assuming round us utterly novel habits, opinions, politics; while the belief that Christ is the same now as he was in Judæa of old—yea, the same yesterday, to-day, and for ever—strives with the plain fact that his field, the world, is in a state in which it never has been since the making of the world; while it is often most difficult, though (as I believe) certainly possible, to see those divine laws at work with which God governed the nations in old time. May God forgive us all, both laity and clergy, every cruel word, every uncharitable thought, every hasty judgment. Have we not need, in such a time as this, of that divine humility which is the elder sister of divine charity? Have we not need of some of that God-inspired modesty of St. Paul's: 'I think as a child, I speak as a child. I see through a glass darkly'? Have we not need to listen to his warning: 'He that regardeth

'the day, to the Lord he regardeth it; and
'he that regardeth it not, to the Lord he
'regardeth it not. Who art thou that judgest
'another? To his own master he standeth
'or falleth. Yea, and he shall stand; for
'God is able to make him stand'? Have
we not need to hear our Lord's solemn
rebuke, when St. John boasted how he saw
one casting out devils in Christ's name, and
he forbade him, because he followed not
them—'Forbid him not'? Have we not
need to believe St. James, when he tells
us that every good gift and every perfect
gift cometh from above, from the Father of
lights, and not (as we have too often fancied)
sometimes from below, from darkness and
the pit? Have we not need to keep in
mind the canon of the wise Gamaliel?—'If
'this counsel or this work be of man, it
'will come to nought: but if it be of God,
'we cannot overthrow it, lest haply we too
'be found fighting even against God.' Have
we not need to keep in mind that 'every
'spirit which confesses that Jesus Christ is
'come in the flesh is of God;' and 'no man

'saith that Jesus is the Christ, save by the 'Spirit of God;' lest haply we, too, be found more fastidious than Almighty God himself? Have we not need to beware lest we, like the Scribes and Pharisees, should be found keeping the key of knowledge, and yet not entering in ourselves, and hindering those who would enter in? Have we not need to beware lest, while we are settling which is the right gate to the kingdom of heaven, the publicans and harlots should press into it before us; and lest, while we are boasting that we are the children of Abraham, God should, without our help, raise up children to Abraham of those stones outside; those hard hearts, dull brains, natures ground down by the drudgery of daily life till they are as the pavement of the streets; those so-called 'heathen masses' of whom we are bid to think this day.

If there be any truth, any reason, in what I have said—or rather in what Christ and his apostles have said—let us lay it to heart upon this day, on which the clergy of this great metropolis have found a common cause for which to plead, whatever may be their minor differences of opinion. Let us wish success to every argument by which this great cause may be enforced, to every scheme of good which may be built up by its funds. Let us remember that, however much the sermons preached this day differ in details, they will all agree, thank God, in the root and ground of their pleading—duty to Christ, and to those for whom Christ died. Let us remember that, to whatever outwardly different purposes the money collected may be applied, it will after all be applied to one purpose—to Christian civilization, Christian teaching, Christian discipline; and that any Christianity, any Christian civilization, any Christian discipline, is infinitely better than none; that, though all man's systems and methods must be imperfect, faulty, yet they are infinitely better than anarchy and heathendom, just as the wheat, however much mixed with weeds, is infinitely better than the weeds alone. But above all, let us wish well to all schemes of education, of whatever kind, certain that any education is better than none. And, therefore, let me entreat you to subscribe bountifully to that scheme for which I specially plead this day.

Let me remind you, very solemnly, that the present dearth of education in these realms is owing mainly to our unhappy religious dissensions; that it is the disputes, not of unbelievers, but of Christians, which have made it impossible for our government to fulfil one of the first rights, one of the first duties, of any government in a civilized country; namely, to command, and to compel, every child in the realm to receive a proper education. Strange and sad that so it should be: yet so it is. We have been letting, we are letting still, year by year, thousands sink and drown in the slough of heathendom and brutality, while we are debating learnedly whether a raft, or a boat, or a rope, or a life-buoy, is the legitimate instrument for saving them; and future historians will record with sorrow and wonder a fact which will be patent to them, though the dust of controversy hides it from our eyes —even the fact that the hinderers of education in these realms were to be found, not among the so-called sceptics, not among the so-called infidels; but among those who believed that God came down from heaven, and became man, and died on the cross, for every savage child in London streets. Compulsory government education is, by our own choice and determination, impossible. The more solemn is the duty laid on us, on laity and clergy alike, to supply that want by voluntary education. The clergy will do their duty, each in his own way. Let the laity do theirs likewise, in fear and trembling, as men who have voluntarily and deliberately undertaken to educate the lower classes; and who must do it, or bear the shame for ever. For in the last day, when we shall all appear before Him whose ways are not as our ways, or his thoughts as our thoughts—in that day, the question will not be, whether the compulsory system, or the denominational system, or any other system, satisfied best our sectarian ways and our narrow thoughts: but whether they satisfied the ways of that Father in heaven who willeth not that one little child should perish.

SERMON. XXIII.

THE KINGDOM OF CHRIST.

LUKE XIX. 41.

And when he was come near, he beheld the city, and wept over it.

LET us think awhile what was meant by our Lord's weeping over Jerusalem. We ought to learn thereby somewhat more of our Lord's character, and of our Lord's government.

Why did he weep over that city whose people would, in a few days, mock him, scourge him, crucify him, and so fill up the measure of their own iniquity? Had Jesus been like too many, who since his time have fancied themselves saints and prophets, would he not have rather cursed the city than wept over it with tenderness, regret, sorrow, most human and most divine, for that horrible destruction which before forty years were past would sweep it off the face of the earth, and leave not one stone of those glorious buildings on another?

The only answer is—that, in spite of all its sins, he loved Jerusalem. For more than a thousand years, he had put his name there. It was to be the salt of the earth, the light of the world, the city set on a hill, which could not be hid. From Jerusalem was to go forth to all nations the knowledge of the one true God, as a light to lighten the Gentiles, as well as a glory to his people Israel.

This was our Lord's purpose; this had been his purpose for one thousand years and more: and behold, man's sin and folly had frustrated for a time the gracious will of God. That glorious city, with its temple, its worship, its religion, true as far as it went, and, in spite of all the traditions with which the Scribes and Pharisees had overlaid it, infinitely better than the creed or religion of any other people in the old world—all this, instead of being a blessing to the world, had become a curse. The Jews, who had the key of the knowledge of God, neither entered in themselves, nor let the Gentiles enter in. They who were to have taught all the world were hating and cursing all the world, and being hated and cursed by them in return. Jerusalem, the Holy City set on a hill, instead of being a light to the world, was become a nuisance to the world. Jerusalem was the salt of the world, meant to help it all from decay; but the salt had lost its savour, and in another generation it would be cast out and trodden under foot, and become a byword among the Gentiles.

Our Lord, The Lord, the hereditary King of the Jews according to the flesh, as well as the God of the Jews according to the Spirit, foresaw the destruction of the work of his own hands, of the spot on earth which was most precious to him. The ruin would be awful, the suffering horrible. The daughters of Jerusalem were to weep, not for him, but for themselves. Blessed would be the barren, and those that never nursed a child. They would call on the mountains to cover them, and on the hills to hide them, and call in vain. Such tribulation would fall on them as never had been since the making of the world. Mothers would eat their own children for famine. Three thousand crosses would stand at one time in the valley below with a living man writhing on each. Eleven hundred thousand souls would perish, or be sold as slaves. It must be. The eternal laws of retribution, according to which God governs the world, must have their way now. It was too late. It must happen now. But it need not have happened: and at that thought our Lord's infinite heart burst forth in human tenderness, human pity, human love, as he looked on that magnificent city, those gorgeous temples, castles, palaces, that mighty multitude which dreamt so little of the awful doom which they were bringing on themselves.

And now, where is he that wept over Jerusalem? Has he left this world to itself? Does he care no longer for the rise and fall of nations, the struggles and hopes, the successes and the failures of mankind?

Not so, my friends. He has ascended up on high, and sat down at the right hand of God: but he has done so, that he might fill all things. To him all power is given in heaven and earth. He reigneth over the nations. He sitteth on that throne whereof the eternal Father hath said to him, 'Sit thou 'on my right hand until I make thy foes thy 'footstool;' and again, 'Desire of me, and I 'shall give thee the heathen for thine inherit-'ance, and the utmost ends of the earth for 'thy possession.' He is set upon his throne (as St. John saw him in his Revelation) judging right, and ministering true judgment unto the people. The nations may furiously rage together, and the people may imagine a vain thing. The kings of the earth may stand up, and the rulers take counsel together, against the Lord, and against his anointed, saying, 'Let us break their bonds'—that is, their laws,—'asunder, and cast away their cords'—that is, their Gospel—'from us.' They may say, 'Tush, God doth not see, neither doth 'God regard it. We are they that ought to 'speak. Who is Lord over us?' Nevertheless Christ is King of kings, and Lord of lords; he reigns, and will reign. And kings must be wise, and the judges of the earth must be learned; they must serve the Lord in fear, and rejoice before him with reverence. They must worship the Son, lest he be angry, and so they perish from the right way. All the nations of the world, with their kings and their people, their war, their trade, their politics, and their arts and sciences, are in his hands as clay in the hands of the potter, fulfilling his will and not their own, going his way and not their own. It is he who speaks concerning a nation or a kingdom, to pluck up, and to pull down, and to destroy it. And it is he again who speaks concerning a nation or kingdom, to build and to plant it. For the Lord is king, be the world never so much moved. He sitteth between the cherubim, though the earth be never so unquiet.

But while we recollect this—which in these days almost all forget—that Christ the Lord is the ruler, and he alone; we must recollect likewise that he is not only a divine, but a human ruler. We must recollect—oh, blessed thought!—that there is a Man in the midst of the throne of heaven; that Christ has taken for ever the manhood into God; and that all judgment is committed to him because he is the Son of man, who can feel for men, and with men.

Yes, Christ's humanity is no less now than when he wept over Jerusalem; and therefore we may believe, we must believe, that while Jesus is very God of very God, yet his sacred heart is touched with a divine compassion for the follies of men, a divine regret for their failures, a divine pity for the ruin which they bring so often on themselves. We must believe that even when he destroys, he does so with regret; that when he cuts down the tree which cumbers the ground, he grieves over it; as he grieved over his chosen vine, the nation of the Jews.

It is a comfort to remember this as we watch the world change, and the fashions of it vanish away. Great kingdoms, venerable institutions, gallant parties, which have done good work in their time upon God's earth, grow old, wear out, lose their first love of what was just and true; and know not the things which belong to their peace, but grow, as the Jews grew in their latter years, more and more fanatical, quarrelsome, peevish, uncharitable; trying to make up by violence for the loss of strength and sincerity: till they come to an end, and die, often by unjust and unfair means, and by men worse than they. Shall we not believe that Christ has pity on them; that he who wept over Jerusalem going to destruction by its own blindness, sorrows over the sins and follies which bring shame on countries once prosperous, authorities once venerable, causes once noble?

They, too, were thoughts of Christ. Whatsoever good was in them, he inspired; whatsoever strength was in them, he gave; whatsoever truth was in them, he taught; whatsoever good work they did, he did through them. Perhaps he looks on them, not with wrath and indignation, but with pity and sorrow, when he sees man's weakness, folly, and sin, bringing to naught his gracious purposes, and falling short of his glorious will.

It is a comfort, I say, to believe this, in these times of change. Places, manners, opinions, institutions, change around us more and more; and we are often sad, when we see good old fashions, in which we were brought up, which we have loved, revered, looked on as sacred things, dying out fast, and new fashions taking their places, which we cannot love because we do not trust them, or even understand. The old ways were good enough for us: why should they not be good enough for our children after us? Therefore, we are sad at times, and the young and the ambitious are apt to sneer at us, because we delight in what is old rather than what is new.

Let us remember, then, that whatsoever changes, still there is one who cannot change, Jesus Christ, the same yesterday, to-day, and for ever. Surely he can feel for us, when he sees us regret old fashions and old times; surely he does not look on our sadness as foolish, weak, or sinful. It is pardonable, for it is human; and he has condescended to feel it himself, when he wept over Jerusalem.

Only, he bids us not despair; not doubt his wisdom, his love, the justice and beneficence of his rule. He ordereth all things in heaven and earth; and, therefore, all things must, at last, go well.

> 'The old order changes, giving place to the new,
> And God fulfils himself in many ways,
> Lest one good custom should corrupt the world.'

We must believe that, and trust in Christ. We must trust in him, that he will not cut down any tree in his garden until it actually cumbers the ground, altogether unfruitful, and taking up room which might be better used. We must trust him, that he will cast nothing out of his kingdom till it actually offends, makes men stumble and fall to their destruction. We must trust him, that he will do away with nothing that is old, without putting something better in its place. Thus we shall keep up our hearts, though things do change round us, sometimes mournfully enough. For Christ destroyed Jerusalem. But, again, its destruction was, as St. Paul said, life to all nations. He destroyed Moses' law. But he, by so doing, put in its place his own Gospel. He scattered abroad the nations of the Jews, but he thereby called into his Church all nations of the earth. He destroyed, with a fearful destruction, the Holy City and temple, over which he wept. But he did so in order that the Holy City, the New Jerusalem, even his Church, should come down from heaven; needing no temple, for he himself is the temple thereof; that the nations of those which were saved should walk in the light of it; and that the river of the water of life should flow from the throne of God; and that the leaves of the trees which grew thereby should be for the healing of the nations. In that magnificent imagery, St. John shows us how the most terrible destruction which the Lord ever brought upon a holy place and holy institutions was really a blessing to all the world. Let us believe that it has been so often since; that it will be so often again. Let us look forward to the future with hope and faith, even while we look back on the past with love and regret. Let us leave unmanly and unchristian fears to those who fancy that Christ has deserted his kingdom, and has left them to govern it in his stead; and who naturally break out into peevishness and terrified lamentations, when they discover that the world will not go their way, or any man's way, because it is going the way of God, whose ways are not as man's ways nor his thoughts as man's thoughts. Let us have faith in God and in Christ, amid all the chances and changes of this mortal life; and believe that he is leading the world and mankind to

> 'One far-off divine event
> Toward which the whole creation moves;'

and possess our souls in patience, and in faith, and in hope for ourselves and for our children after; while we say, with the Psalmist of old: "Thou, Lord, in the be-
' ginning hast laid the foundations of the
' earth, and the heavens are the work of thy
' hands. They shall perish, but thou shalt
' endure. They all shall wax old as doth a
' garment; and as a vesture shalt thou change
' them, and they shall be cleansed. But thou

'art the same, and thy years shall not fail.
'The children of thy servants shall con-
'tinue; and their seed shall stand fast in
'thy sight.' Amen.

SERMON XXIV.

THE LIKENESS OF GOD.

EPHESIANS IV. 23, 24.

And be renewed in the spirit of your mind; and that ye put on the new man, which after God is created in righteousness and true holiness.

BE renewed, says St. Paul, in the spirit of your mind—in the tone, character, and habit of your mind. And put on the new man, the new pattern of man, who was created after God, in righteousness and true holiness.

Pay attention, I beg you, to every word here. To understand them clearly is most important to you. According as you take them rightly or wrongly, will your religion be healthy or unhealthy, and your notion of what God requires of you true or false. The new man, the new pattern of man, says St. Paul, is created after God. That, is after the pattern of God, in the image of God, in the likeness of God. You will surely see that that is his meaning. We speak of making a thing after another thing; meaning, to make it exactly like another thing. So, by making a man after God, St. Paul means making a man like God.

Now what is this man? None, be sure, save Christ himself, the co-equal and co-eternal Son of God. Of him alone can it be said, utterly, that he is after God—the brightness of God's glory, and the express image of his person. But still, he is a man, and meant as a pattern to men; the new Adam; the new pattern, type, and ideal for all mankind. Him, says St. Paul,—that is, his likeness,—we are to put on, that as he was after the likeness of God, so may we be likewise.

But now, in what does this same likeness consist?

St. Paul tells us distinctly, lest we should mistake a matter of such boundless importance as the question of all questions—What is the life of God, the Divine and Godlike life?

It is created, founded, says he, in **righteousness and true holiness**. That is the character, that is the form of it. Whatever we do not know, whatever we cannot know, concerning God, and his Divine life, we know that it consists of righteousness and true holiness.

And what is righteousness? Justice. You must understand—as any good scholar or divine would assure you—that St. Paul is not speaking here of the imputed righteousness of Christ. He is speaking of righteousness in the simple Old Testament meaning of the word, of justice, whereof our Lord has said, 'Do unto others as ye would they should do unto you;' justice, which, as wise men of old have said, consists in this,—to harm no man, and to give each man his own. That is true righteousness and justice, and that is the Godlike life.

'And true holiness.' That is, truthful holiness, honest holiness. This is St. Paul's meaning. As any good scholar or divine would tell you, St. Paul's exact words are, 'the holiness of truth.' He does not mean true holiness as opposed to a false holiness, a legal holiness, a holiness of empty forms and ceremonies, or a holinesss of ascetism and celibacy; but as opposed to a holiness which does not speak the truth, to that sly, untruthful, prevaricating holiness which was only too common in St. Paul's time, and has been but too common since. Be honest, says St. Paul; for this too is part of the Godlike life, and the new man is created after God, in justice and honesty.

And that this is what St. Paul actually means is clear from what immediately follows: 'Wherefore, putting away lying, speak every 'man truth with his neighbour: for we are 'members one of another.'

What does the 'wherefore' mean, if not that, because the life of God is a life of justice and honesty, therefore you must not lie; therefore you must not bear spite and malice; therefore you must not steal, but rather work; therefore you must avoid all foul talk which may injure your neighbour; but rather teach, refine, educate him?

It would seem at first sight that this would have been a gospel, and good news to men.

But, alas! it has not been such. In all ages, in all religions, men have turned away from this simple righteousness of God, which is created in justice and truth, and have sought some righteousness of their own, founded upon anything and everything save common morality and honesty. Alas for the spiritual pride of man! He is not content to be simply just and true! for any one and every one, he thinks, can be that. He must needs be something, which other people cannot be. He must needs be able to thank God that he is not as other men are, and say, 'This people, this 'wicked world, who knoweth not our law, is 'accursed.'

If God had bid men do some great thing to save their souls, would they not have done it? How much more when he says simply to them, as to Naaman, 'Wash, and be clean.' 'Wash you,' says the Lord by the prophet Isaiah, 'make you clean. Put away the evil 'of your doings from before my eyes. Cease 'to do evil. Learn to do well, seek justice, 'relieve the oppressed,' and then, 'though 'your sins be as scarlet, they shall be white 'as snow.' But no: any one can do that; and therefore it is beneath the spiritual pride of man. In our own days, there are too many who do not hesitate to look down on plain justice, and plain honesty, as natural virtues, which (so they say) men can have without the grace of God, and make a distinction between these natural virtues and the effects of God's Spirit; which is not only not to be found in Scripture, but is contradicted by Scripture from beginning to end.

Now there can be no doubt that such notions concerning religion do harm; that they demoralise thousands,—that is, make them less moral and good men. For there are thousands, especially in England, who are persons of good common-sense, uprightness, and truthfulness: but they have not lively fancies, or quick feelings. They have no inclination for a life of exclusive devoutness; and if they had, they have no time for it. They must do their business in the world where God has put them. And when they are told that God requires of them certain frames and feelings, and that the Godlike life consists in them, then they are disheartened, and say, 'There is no use, then, in my trying 'to be religious, or moral either. If plain 'honesty, justice, sobriety, usefulness in my 'place will not please God, I cannot please 'him at all. Why then should I try, if my 'way of trying is of no use? Why should I 'try to be honest, sober, and useful, if that is 'not true religion?—if what God wants of 'me is not virtue, but a certain high-flown 'religiousness which I cannot feel or even 'understand?'—and so they grow weary in well-doing, and careless about the plain duties of morality. They become careless, likewise, about the plain duties of religion; and so they are demoralised, because they are told that justice and the holiness of truth are not the Godlike and eternal life; because they are told that religion has little or nothing to do with their daily life and business, nothing to do with those just and truthful instincts of their hearts, which they feel to be the most sacred things about them; which are their best, if not their only guide in life. But more: they fall into the mistake that they can have a righteousness of their own; and into that Pelagianism, as it is called, which is growing more and more the creed of modern men of the world.

Too many religious people, on the other hand, are demoralised by the very same notion.

They too are taught that justice and truth are mere 'morality,' as it is called, and not the grace of God; that they are not the foundation of the Divine life, that they are not the essence of true religion. Therefore they become more and more careless about mere morality,—so careless of justice, so careless of truth, as to bring often fearful scandals on religion.

Meanwhile men in general, especially Englishmen, have a very sound instinct on this whole matter. They have a sound instinct that if God be good, then goodness is the only true mark of godliness; and that goodness consists first and foremost in plain justice and plain honesty; and they ask, not what a man's religious profession is, not what his religious observances are: but—'What is the 'man himself? Is he a just, upright, and fair-dealing man? Is he true? Can we depend 'on his word?' If not, his religion counts for nothing with them: as it ought to count.

Now I hold that St. Paul in this text declares that the plain English folk who talk thus, and who are too often called mere worldlings, and men of the world, are right; that justice and honesty are the Divine life itself, and the very likeness of Christ and of God.

Justice and truth all men can have, and therefore all men are required to have. About devotional feelings, about religious observances, however excellent and blessed, we may deceive ourselves; for we may put them in the place of sanctification, of righteousness and true holiness. About justice and honesty we cannot deceive ourselves; for they are sanctification itself, righteousness itself, true holiness itself, the very likeness of God, and the very grace of God.

But if so, they come from God; they are God's gift, and not any natural product of our own hearts: and for that very reason we can and must keep them alive in us by prayer. As long as we think that the sentiment of justice and truth is our own, so long shall we be in danger of forgetting it, paltering with it, playing false to it in temptation, and by some injustice or meanness grieving (as St. Paul warns us) the Holy Spirit of God, who has inspired us with that priceless treasure.

But if we believe that from God, the fount of justice, comes all our justice; that from God, the fount of truth, comes all our truthfulness, then we shall cry earnestly to him, day by day, as we go about this world's work, to be kept from all injustice, and from all falsehood. We shall entreat him to cleanse us from our secret faults, and to give us truth in the inward parts; to pour into our hearts that love to our neighbour which is justice itself, for it worketh no ill to its neighbour, and so fulfils the law. We shall dread all meanness and cruelty, as sins against the very Spirit of God; and our most earnest and solemn endeavour in life will be, to keep innocence, and take heed to the thing that is right; for that will bring us peace at the last.